Praise for Richard Lederer

"Columnist and punster Richard Lederer may be William Safire's only living peer at writing about grammar, word usage, and derivations."
—*Washington Post Book World*

"Lederer beguiles and bedazzles."
—*Los Angeles Times*

"Richard Lederer is the true King of Language Comedy."
—Sidney Sheldon, author of *After the Darkness*

"Columnist Extraordinaire."
—*The New Yorker*

"Richard Lederer opens the treasure chest of English and delights in each shiny coin he finds."
—Rob Kyff, author of *Once Upon a Word*

"Richard Lederer's delight in English is itself delightful and contagious!"
—Edwin Newman, author of *Strictly Speaking* and *A Civil Tongue*

"Richard Lederer ought to be declared a national treasure."
—*Richmond Times-Dispatch*

"Richard Lederer has outdone Richard Lederer."
—Paul Dickson, author of *What's in a Name?*

"Wordplay that's fast, furious, and funny."
—Will Shortz, crossword editor, *The New York Times*

"Is there anyone alive who has more fun with the English language than Richard Lederer?"
—Charles Harrington Elster, author of *Word Workout*

"America's Wizard of Idiom."
—*Denver Post*

THE JOY OF NAMES

THE JOY OF NAMES

Mary · James · Chloe · Ira · Liam · Tavonda · Noah · Gary · Mohammad · Sophia · Emma · Adam · Ava

RICHARD LEDERER

Illustrated by Todd Smith

Marion Street Press

Portland, Oregon

To Ted Croll, transcend-dental verbivore

Acknowledgments

Deepest thanks to Caroline McCullagh, my long-time writing partner and invaluable researcher for this book, and to Don Hauptman, Stan Kegel, and Bonnie Wilpon for providing examples for "The Lighter Side of Names." Surpassing gratitude to my illustrious illustrator Todd Smith, who, uncannily, draws the way I think. The chapters "What's in a President's Name?" and "Pen-Ultimate Names" are adapted from my *Presidential Trivia* and *Literary Trivia* (Gibbs Smith 2017 and 2007).

Published by Marion Street Press, LLC
4207 SE Woodstock Blvd # 168
Portland, OR 97206-6267
USA
http://www.marionstreetpress.com/

Orders and review copies: (800) 888-4741

Printed in the United States of America
ISBN 9781933338361

Back cover photo by Hoffman Photographic

Library of Congress CIP Data pending

Contents

Introduction

Every person has a name. Every name has a story behind it.
And every story behind a name has a cultural context
in which it is embedded.

—HALEY LISA CLOSE

I, Richard Henry Lederer (which means "powerful estate ruler leather worker"), will bet the farm, my bippie, and my bottom dollar that you, valued reader, have a name. I'm confident about that assertion because almost all human beings do, and that name makes up a part of your identity—who you are and how the world sees you.

One of the first things that you acquired when you entered this world was your name. Nothing is more personal to you. You carry it everywhere as a badge of your individuality and uniqueness. No one else in the history of humanity has used the same voice as you to speak your name. And "What's your name?" is perhaps the most common question you ask and answer when you meet a stranger.

Your name possesses the secret power to call you. A number of studies show that babies can recognize their names as young as four-and-a-half months and that a person can clearly hear his or her name spoken across a crowded, noisy room.

New England poet James Russell Lowell, observed, "There is more force in names than most men dream of." Lewis Carroll recognized this force when he wrote in *Through the Looking-Glass, and What Alice Found There*:

"My name is Alice. . . ."

"It's a stupid name enough!" Humpty Dumpty interrupted impatiently. "What does it mean?"

"Must a name mean something?" Alice asked doubtfully.

"Of course it must," Humpty Dumpty said with a short laugh. "My name means the shape I am—and a good handsome shape it is, too. With a name like yours, you might be any shape, almost."

ix

Dumpty is wrong in one respect. The name *Alice* does have a meaning; it means "nobility." But the egghead (soon to be an omelet) is perfectly correct when he eggs Alice on with "My name means the shape I am." Our name indeed gives us a "shape."

This practice of naming is rooted in ancient creation stories. According to the Mayan sacred book *Popol Vuh,* after the Creators made the earth; carved its mountains, valleys, and rivers; and swathed it with vegetation; they formed the animals who would be guardians of the plant world and who would praise the Makers' names: "'Speak, then, our names, praise us, your mother, your father. Invoke, then, Huracan, Chipi-Caculha, the Heart of Heaven, the Heart of Earth, the Creators, the Makers, the Forefathers. Speak, invoke us, adore us.'

"But the animals only hissed and screamed and cackled. They were unable to make words, and each screamed in a different way. When the Creators and the Makers saw that it was impossible for them to talk to each other, they said: 'It is impossible for them to say the names of us, their Creators and Makers. This is not well.' As a punishment, the birds and animals were condemned to be eaten and sacrificed by others, and the Creators set out to make another creature who would be able to call their names and speak their praises. This creature was man and woman."

In the creation story that so majestically begins the Bible (Genesis 1:1-31, 2:1-6), we note the frequency and importance of verbs of speaking and naming: "And God *said,* Let there be light; and there was light. . . . And God *called* the light Day, and the darkness he *called* Night. . . . And God *said,* Let there be a firmament in the midst of the waters. . . . And God *called* the firmament Heaven." [Emphases mine.] The italicized verbs above tell us that God doesn't just snap his fingers to bring the things of the universe into existence. He speaks them into being and then names each one.

Here's what happens when God creates Adam: "And out of the ground the lord God formed every beast of the field, and every fowl of the air; and brought them unto Adam to see what he would call them; and whatsoever Adam called every living creature, that was the name thereof" (Genesis 2:19-22). In other words, Adam (Hebrew for "the first man") does what God has done: He names things; he names voraciously; he names *everything.* Perhaps this is what the Bible means in Genesis 1:26-27: "And God said, Let us make man in our own image, after our likeness. . . . So God created man in his own image, in the image of God created he him, male and female created he them."

Like God, man is a speaker and a namer.

Both creation stories sing the human desire and power to name everything. And these qualities that define our humanness are nowhere better exhibited than in our desire and power to name ourselves.

The ancient Greek philosopher Antisthenes observed, "The beginning of all instruction is the study of names." That study is called onomastics, from the Greek *onomastikós*, "of or belonging to names."

The Joy of Names is not a book about the names we give to places, flowers, ships, pets, and other animals. Rather, the focus in the pages that follow will be on human names, the names we bestow upon ourselves and our fictional creations. The fancy title for that area is anthroponymy: Greek *anthropo* = "human," + *nym* = "name."

The oldest name that we know is that of Kushim, a Sumerian who signed a cuneiform receipt for 29,086 measures of barley. The voucher, a clay tablet created circa 3200 BCE, was found with thousands of others in modern-day Iraq, formerly known as Mesopotamia.

The next oldest names on record are those of Gal-Sal and two slaves he or she owned, En-pap X and Sukkalgir, also in Mesopotamia, probably a hundred years or so after Kushim.

Some might argue that Adam is the most ancient of names and Eve the second most, but Kushim, Gal-Sal, En-pap X, and Sukkalgir are the first names we know that were written down at the time the named people were alive.

In the first part of this book, "What's in a Name?," you'll find out how first names came about and what they mean, why we acquired last names and nicknames and what they mean, how to name your precious baby, how and why authors and movie and television stars change their names, hidden patterns of presidents' names, how proper names from history and literature become lowercase words that populate our everyday vocabulary, and a gallery of cruel and unusual names.

In the second cluster, "The Lighter Side of Names," you'll step right up to a three ring-a-ding circus of names—names swinging from tent-tops, names teetering on tightropes, names swallowing swords and breathing fire, names leaping through flaming hoopla, names somersaulting heels over head, sideshow names with shapes beyond the arena of ordinary life, names going for the juggler! I guarantee that all the humor will be in tents.

Almost every chapter in this book includes a Name Game or two or three, three dozen in all. Any good game consists of items of varying levels of difficulty. Some of the posers are likely to stump you the first time around. Don't give up. You will find that solutions to the more challenging questions will come to you in sudden flashes of insight when you return to the game. When you are sure that you have tried your best, proceed to the answers.

But even if you turn your nose up at games and plan to skip them, you can still drink deeply from the well of knowledge and humor in these pages.

Richard Lederer
richardhlederer@gmail.com
www.verbivore.com

WHAT'S IN A NAME?

What's in a name? That which we call a rose
By any other name would smell as sweet.
—WILLIAM SHAKESPEARE

I think squash would taste better
if it had a different name.
—BILLY IN *THE FAMILY CIRCUS*, BY JEFF AND BILL KEANE

In real life, unlike in Shakespeare,
the sweetness of the rose depends upon the name it bears.
Things are not only what they are.
They are, in very important respects, what they seem to be.
—HUBERT HUMPHREY

What's in a name, really?
Does a rose by any other name really smell as sweet?
Would the most famous love story in the world be as poignant
if it was called Romeo and Gertrude?
Why is what we call ourselves so important?
—JULIE KAGAWA

It may be that which we call a rose
by any other name would smell as sweet,
but I should be loath to see a rose on a maiden's breast
substituted by a flower, however beautiful and fragrant it might be,
that went by the name skunk lily.
—ALEX HENRY

What's in a name?
The accumulation of reputations
from all who've owned it before you.
—RICHELLE E. GOODRICH

First Names First

Teddy Bear

The bestowal of a name and identity is a kind of symbolic contract
by the society and the individual. Seen from one side of the contract,
by giving a name the society confirms the individual's existence
and acknowledges its responsibilities toward that person.
The name differentiates the child from others.
Thus, the society will be able to treat and deal with the child
as someone with needs and feelings different from those of other people.
—H. EDWARD DELUZAIN

Names are an important key to what a society values.
Anthropologists recognize naming as one of the chief methods
of imposing order on perception.
—DAVID SLAWSON

I have fallen in love with American names,
The sharp, gaunt names that never get fat.
—STEPHEN VINCENT BENET

In 1989, the United Nations General Assembly adopted a resolution titled Rights of the Child, which includes the statement "Every child has the right from birth to a name."

A child is born physically into the world by the mother, but the child is also born into his or her social group by the process of naming. In some communities children are not considered to be socially alive until they are given a name.

In every society around the world, naming is vital and is usually accompanied by ceremony. Among Christians, it is at baptism that the child receives his or her Christian name. Muslims perform a baby-naming ceremony on the seventh day after birth. Although most Muslims are not Arabs, it's common for babies to receive Arabic names. Jews celebrate the naming of a baby boy on the eighth day after birth at the bris (circumcision) ritual, when he receives his Hebrew name. Jewish girls are welcomed and receive their Hebrew names in b'rit bat ceremonies, usually thirty days after birth.

Not only is the fact of naming important, the name itself may have social implications across the society or through time. In some cultures, a person's name weaves him or her into a web of responsibility to all other people with the same name. In others, ancestors with the same name shield or hide the child from vengeful spirits.

Before the Norman Conquest of Britain in A.D. 1066, people were not identified by hereditary surnames. They were known just by a personal name or nickname. John was the most common personal name in English-speaking countries for many centuries. In England during the Middle Ages, John was bestowed upon approximately one fifth of English boys.

The first name (also called "a given name") John descends from the Hebrew Yochanan and can be translated as either "Gift of God" or "God is gracious." In the United States over the past century (1917–2016), John has been the second most popular boys' name, after James.

Around the world we find many variations of John: Evan (Welsh), Giannis (Greek), Giovanni (Italian), Gjon (Albanian), Hanna (Arabic), Hans(el) (Danish, Dutch, and German), Hovhannes (Armenian), Ian (Scottish), Iban (Basque), Ivan (Russian), Ivo (Croatian), Jack (English), Jan (Belgian, Dutch, and Polish), Janek (Czech), Jannis (Latvian), Janos (Hungarian), Jean (French), Jens (Swedish), Joan (Catalan). João (Portuguese), Johann(es) (German and Norwegian), Jonas (Lithuanian), Juan (Spanish), Juhan (Estonian), Ohannes (Turkish), Sean and Shane (Irish), Vania (Serbian), and Yanko (Bulgarian).

Turning to the distaff side, Elizabeth, that popular, royal English name that means "consecrated of God," sparks forth more derivative names than any other first name—Babette, Bess, Bessie, Bessy, Bet, Beth, Bethina, Betsey, Betsy, Betta, Bette, Bettie, Bettina, Bettine, Betty, Bettye, Buffy, Elisa, Elisabet, Elise, Elissa, Elisse, Eliza, Ella, Elle, Ellie, Elly, Elsa, Else, Elsie, Elyse, Ilse, Leanna, Leanne, Leesa, Liana, Lib, Libbie, Libby, Liddy, Lil, Liliana, Lillia, Lillian, Lillie, Lilo, Lily, Lilybet, Lilybeth, Lis, Lisa, Lisabet, Lisabeth, Lisbet, Lisbeth, Lise, Lisette, Lissa, Liz, Liza, Lizabeth, Lizbet, Lizbeth, Lize, Lizette, Lizolet, Lizza, Lizzie, Lizzy, and Lyssa. That's more than seventy Elizabethan transmutations.

At one time or another, almost everyone has wondered, "What does my name mean?" Most given names possess meaning because people often derive first names from their physical or social world. Thus, Eugene means "well born" and Stella "a star." Here are a hundred and fifty more given names with their meanings:

Adam: earth, the first man
Albert: noble, bright
Alexander: defending warrior
Austin: great, magnificent

Abigail: My father exalts
Alma: nourishing
Anne: favored by God
Barbara: foreign

Benedict: blessed

Benjamin: son of the south

Bernard: brave as a bear

Bradley: broad clearing

Carmen: song

Charles: free man

Damon: to tame

Daniel: God is my judge

David: beloved, friend

Dexter: right-handed, auspicious

Dominic: lord

Donald: ruler of the world

Edward: prosperous guardian

Elijah: The Lord is my God

Ethan: strong, firm

Francis: Frenchman

Frederick: peaceful ruler

Gary: spear

George: farmer

Gerald: rule of the spear

Gilbert: bright pledge

Glenn: valley

Gregory: watchful

Harold: army leader

Harvey: battleworthy

Hayden: hay valley

Henry: home ruler

Herbert: army bright

Howard: high guardian

Ira: watchful

Isaac: to laugh

Jason: to heal

James: supplanter

Joseph: Jehovah will add

Joshua: God is salvation

Kenneth: handsome

Kirk: church

Leo: lion

Beatrice: blessed voyager

Blanche: white, fair

Bonita: pretty

Catherine: fertility

Chloe: green shoot

Colleen: girl

Danika: morning star

Daphne: laurel

Darlene: darling

Deborah: bee

Diana: moon goddess

Dorothy: gift of God

Emily: industrious

Emma: whole, entire

Esther: star

Eve: alive

Fay: fairy

Florence: flourishing

Gloria: glory

Hazel: light brown

Helen: sunbeam, the bright one

Hillary: cheerful

Ida: work, labor

Irene: peace

Irma: whole, entire

Isabelle: beautiful

Jennifer: fair, white

Jessica: God beholds

Judith: woman from Judea

Kirsten: bearing Christ

Laura: laurel

Leah: weary

Leila: night

Leslie: garden of holly

Linda: beautiful

Lorraine: laurel

Lucy: light

Margaret: pearl

Lloyd: gray

Matthew: gift of God

Michael: who is like God

Milton: mill town

Mohamed: praiseworthy

Nathan: He gives

Neil: champion

Nicholas: victory of the people

Noah: rest, comfort

Norman: Northman, Viking

Patrick: nobleman

Peter: a rock

Philip: lover of horses

Raymond: wise protector

Rex: king

Richard: powerful

Robert: bright fame

Roger: famous spear

Roosevelt: rose field

Roy: king

Ryan: little king

Samuel: God has hearkened

Shaquille: handsome

Solomon: peace

Spencer: dispenser of provisions

Stephen: garland, crown

Stuart: house guard

Theodore: gift of God

Thomas: twin

Timothy: honored by God

Todd: fox

Vincent: conquering

William: determined helmet

Martha: lady

Matilda: strength in battle

Mary: star of the sea

Megan: pearl

Mildred: gentle strength

Miranda: admirable

Morgan: sea horse

Nancy: gracious

Naomi: pleasant one

Natalie: Christmas day

Patricia: noblewoman

Paula: small, humble

Phyllis: foliage, green

Rebecca: join together

Regina: queen

Rhoda: rose

Rhonda: good spear

Rosalind: beautiful rose

Ruth: friendship

Sarah: princess

Serena: tranquil

Shirley: bright clearing

Sophia: wisdom

Susan: lily, rose

Sylvia: of the woods

Tanisha: alive, healthy

Theresa: reaper

Tiffany: appearance of God

Vera: truth

Veronica: true image

Whitney: white island

Yoko: good girl

Yolanda: violet flower

First names, like last names, may evolve into common words when they are used in a general sense. Consider the beloved teddy bear: While hunting in Mississippi in November 1902, President Theodore Roosevelt spared the life of a bear cub. Ever since, the stuffed toys have borne the affectionate form of his first name. Roosevelt used the bear as a symbol in his successful 1904 presidential election, and in 1906 *teddy's bear* entered the dictionary, where it has remained ever since but has shed its possessive ending. Now, more than a century later, children still hug their adorable teddy bears.

In medieval times it was considered great sport to watch the antics of insane people in asylums, such as Bedlam in London. The nicknames Tom o'Bedlam and Tom's Fool were often used for male inmates who were favorites of the gallery or who were released from custody with a license to beg. *Tomfoolery* nowadays simply means "nonsense, silly behavior."

The bobbies of London are named for Sir Robert Peel, who, as Home Secretary, established London's Metropolitan Police in 1829. Early on, they were also called *peelers*, but that name faded away in favor of *bobbies*.

The adjective *tawdry* is a clipping and joining of *(Sain)t Audrey*, the patron saint of Ely, in England. On Saint Audrey's birthday, October 17, the people of Ely traditionally held a fair at which flashy jewelry, knickknacks, and lace were sold. Cheap finery came to be associated with Saint Audrey, and the adjective *tawdry* has been extended to mean anything cheap and gaudy in appearance or quality.

Name Game

The statements in the quiz that follows concern words that contain parts that sound like first names. In most cases, the word actually descends from the first name given. Let's start with *Jack*-words. Legend tells us that a notorious drinker named Jack was too miserly for heaven and excluded from hell for tweaking the Devil with practical jokes. Until Judgment Day, Jack is condemned to wander the earth with a lantern carved from a turnip. (The pumpkin with its fiery grin is an American adaptation.) And that's where we get our word *jack-o'-lantern*.

Show that you're a smart aleck by identifying more *Jack*-words. *Jack* may appear at the beginning or end of an answer:

1. This Jack is a large hare.
2. This Jack is stubborn as a mule.
3. This Jack is for the birds.

4. This Jack is a wild African dog.
5. This Jack is a flower.
6. This Jack is sharp and cutting.
7. This Jack pops up all over.
8. This Jack is extremely versatile.
9. This Jack is a big win.
10. This Jack can shatter concrete.
11. This Jack can hit you hard.
12. This Jack tastes good for breakfast.
13. This Jack can see the trees for the forest.
14. This Jack is a pick-up stick.
15. This Jack takes the plane.
16. This Jack is strong enough to lift cars.
17. This Jack has you up its sleeves.
18. This Jack is a misbehaving boy.
19. This Jack gets the boot.
20. This Jack is wonderful!

Now show that you're a jack-of-all-trades and Johnny-on-the-spot by identifying words that contain variations of the names *Bob, Tom, John, Bill,* and *Jim*:

21. This Bob is a whiz on snowy hills.
22. This Bob girls wore on their feet.
23. This Bob girls wear in their hair.
24. This Bob is a hairstyle.
25. This Bob is a North American lynx.
26. This Bob is for the birds.
27. This Bob is for the birds, too.
28. This Bob is a nag.
29. This Bob is spinner.
30. This Tom is the cat's meow.
31. This Tom is a son of a gun.
32. This Tom is Native American.
33. This Tom is a girl.
34. This Tom kids around a lot.
35. This Tom is utter nonsense.
36. This Tom keeps up the beat.

37. This John keeps us warm in winter.
38. This John is a flower.
39. This John tastes as good as flapjacks.
40. This John we visit several times a day.
41. This Bill is powerfully striking.
42. This Bill can get your goat.
43. This Bill heads for the hills.
44. This Bill plays games.
45. This Bill makes waves.
46. This Bill looks better than a million dollars.
47. This Jim loves ice cream.
48. This Jim can open safes.
49. This Jim has the jitters.
50. This Jim is wonderful!

Answers

1. jackrabbit 2. jackass 3. jackdaw 4. jackal 5. jack-in-the-pulpit 6. jack-knife 7. jack-in-the-box 8. jack-of-all-trades 9. jackpot 10. jackhammer

11. blackjack 12. flapjack 13. lumberjack 14. jackstraw 15. hijack 16. jack 17. jacket 18. jackanapes 19. bootjack or jackboot 20. crackerjack

21. bobsled 22. bobby socks 23. bobby pin 24. bobbed hair 25. bobcat 26. bobolink 27. bobwhite 28. bobtail 29. bobbin 30. tomcat

31. tommy gun 32. tomahawk 33. tomboy 34. tomfoolery 35. tommyrot 36. tom-tom 37. long johns 38. johnny-jump-up 39. johnnycake 40. the john

41. billy club 42. billy goat 43. hillbilly 44. billiards 45. billow 46. a billion 47. jimmies 48. jimmy 49. jimjams 50. jim-dandy

It's a Boy! It's a Girl! It's a Name!

A name can't begin to encompass the sum of all her parts.
But that's the magic of names, isn't it?
That the complex, contradictory individuals we are
can be called up complete and whole
in another mind through the simple sorcery of a name.
—CHARLES DELINT

Names turned over by time, like the plough turning the soil.
Bringing up the new while the old were buried in the mud.
—JOE ABERCROMBIE

I hate guys named Todd. I think that's a goofy name.
All the boys' names that have come along—
Taylor, Tucker, Carlson, Cassidy, Cody, Flynn—
they're not real names. A real name is Jim.
—GEORGE CARLIN

We named all our children Kid.
Well, they have different first names,
like Hey Kid, You Kid, Dumb Kid.
—PHYLLIS DILLER

A name is the first gift that parents give to their children. Choosing a new baby's name is one of the joyous jobs that come with being a mom or a dad.

In bygone days, parents-to-be didn't have to think much about what they were going to name their babies. They figured they would either name their child after one of them or after a favored relative or bestow upon him or her one of the names that were in fashion, more often than not a name of religious origin.

Today, times have changed because we have changed. The number of first names to choose from has vastly multiplied, in large part because of the bazillions of baby-naming books now on the market and the internet.

According to the Official U.S. Social Security Administration list, here are the fifty most popular first names for male and female babies born 1930–39. Yours truly became one of those babies in 1938:

1.	Robert	Mary
2.	James	Betty
3.	John	Barbara
4.	William	Shirley
5.	Richard	Patricia
6.	Charles	Dorothy
7.	Donald	Joan
8.	George	Margaret
9.	Thomas	Nancy
10.	Joseph	Helen
11.	David	Carol
12.	Edward	Joyce
13.	Ronald	Doris
14.	Paul	Ruth
15.	Kenneth	Virginia
16.	Frank	Marilyn
17.	Raymond	Elizabeth
18.	Jack	Jean

19.	Harold	Frances
20.	Billy	Beverly
21.	Gerald	Lois
22.	Walter	Alice
23.	Jerry	Donna
24.	Joe	Martha
25.	Eugene	Dolores
26.	Henry	Janet
27.	Bobby	Phyllis
28.	Arthur	Norma
29.	Carl	Carolyn
30.	Larry	Evelyn
31.	Ralph	Gloria
32.	Albert	Anna
33.	Willie	Marie
34.	Fred	Ann
35.	Michael	Mildred
36.	Lawrence	Rose
37.	Harry	Peggy
38.	Howard	Geraldine
39.	Roy	Catherine
40.	Norman	Judith
41.	Roger	Louise
42.	Daniel	Janice
43.	Louis	Marjorie
44.	Earl	Annie
45.	Gary	Ruby
46.	Clarence	Eleanor
47.	Anthony	Jane
48.	Francis	Sandra
49.	Wayne	Irene
50.	Marvin	Wanda

Now have a look at the Social Security line-up of the top names for boys and girls in 2016, the last full year I had access to when I cobbled together this book:

1.	Noah	Emma
2.	Liam	Olivia
3.	William	Ava
4.	Mason	Sophia
5.	James	Isabella
6.	Benjamin	Mia
7.	Jacob	Charlotte
8.	Michael	Abigail
9.	Elijah	Emily
10.	Ethan	Harper
11.	Alexander	Amelia
12.	Oliver	Evelyn
13.	Daniel	Elizabeth
14.	Lucas	Sofia
15.	Matthew	Madison
16.	Aiden	Avery
17.	Jackson	Ella
18.	Logan	Scarlett
19.	David	Grace
20.	Joseph	Chloe
21.	Samuel	Victoria
22.	Henry	Riley
23.	Owen	Aria
24.	Sebastian	Lily
25.	Gabriel	Aubrey
26.	Carter	Zoey
27.	Jayden	Penelope
28.	John	Lillian
29.	Luke	Addison
30.	Anthony	Layla
31.	Isaac	Natalie
32.	Dylan	Camilia
33.	Wyatt	Hannah
34.	Andrew	Brooklyn
35.	Joshua	Zoe
36.	Christopher	Nora
37.	Grayson	Leah
38.	Jack	Savannah

39. Julian	Audrey
40. Ryan	Claire
41. Jaxon	Eleanor
42. Levi	Skylar
43. Nathan	Ellie
44. Caleb	Samantha
45. Hunter	Stella
46. Christian	Paisley
47. Isaiah	Violet
48. Thomas	Mila
49. Aaron	Allison
50. Lincoln	Alexa

What conclusions can we reach by comparing the 1930s and 2016 lists?

It's a brave new baby-naming world out there. The times they are a changin', and so are tastes. Parents' preferences for baby names swing with the times.

The most striking comparison is that, of the top twenty boys' names in the 1930s record, only seven appear in the 2016 top fifty! Robert, the most popular name in the Thirties, has been demoted from the pinnacle to sixty-two. My first name, Richard, is one of the most enduringly successful Old French names infused into English by the Normans. Its popularity was boosted by the fact that three English kings have borne that name. But—weep weep, sob sob, honk honk!—Richard has free fallen from fifth place in the 1930s line-up to one hundred and sixty in 2016.

Of the first twenty girls' names in the Thirties, Elizabeth is the only one to have survived the passage of almost fourscore years, moving from the seventeenth position to the thirteenth. Mary, the most popular 1930s name for girls, has descended to one-hundred-and twenty-seventh, and seven of the top twenty female names from the Thirties do not reside even among the top thousand choices in 2016!

One contributor to this attrition is that families are less frequently naming their children after parents or earlier ancestors or saints. Boys' names used to change very little over time because a great many fathers thought like Mr. Dombey in Charles Dickens's *Dombey and Son:* "He will be christened Paul, of course. His father's name, Mrs. Dombey, and his grandfather's."

We are a much more diverse nation than we were in the Thirties, and that vector is reflected in the declining uniformity of baby first names.

The 2016 list is more ethnic and international and less predominantly western European than the 1930s list.

The 2016 list includes more names that are relatively new, unusual, and unique to such collections. The Social Security Administration lists keep adding new creations. That's because the pool of names for babies is becoming ever wider and deeper as parents grow ever more adventuresome and individual in their tastes. And these expectant moms and dads have, through internet and real-world lists access to a much greater menu of names from which to choose.

As a result, fewer and fewer children receive one of the Top Ten names. In 1900, fully *half* of babies did. In the 1930s, about one quarter did. Today the percentage is 7.5. These days there is nothing unusual about unusual names. Today's parents value uniqueness over conformity; explains research psychologist Jean Twenge, "Parents are now more likely to want their children to stand out rather than to fit in."

I'm no expert in newborn naming, but that doesn't stop me from presenting a dozen decisions to consider when naming your baby:

• **Namesakes**. Honoring a beloved elder in your family is admirable, but the practice can lead to unfortunate name choices. Names like Bertha, Beulah, Ethel, Gertrude, Hortense, Mabel, Mildred, Priscilla, and Wanda don't fit a little girl comfortably these days, although they're fine for your eighty-five-year-old great aunt. Ask yourself how will Bertha or Ethel feel in a classroom of Scarletts and Madisons?

• **Gender**. Beware and be wary of choosing names that can be given to boys and girls alike, such as Beverly/Beverley, Carol/Carroll, Leigh/Lee, Leslie/Lesley, Avery, Chris, Kim, Marion, Robin, Shirley, and Terry. It can be psychologically scarring to require a child to explain which gender he or she is. (Remember the song "A Boy Named Sue"?) Androgynous names are generally harder on boys than on girls.

But here's another twist: In his *New York Times* magazine language column, William Safire wrote, "Androgynous names abound. Ashley used to be a boy's name, as fans of *Gone with the Wind* remember. (Ashley Wilkes was played by Leslie Howard; now even Leslie is a girl's name.) Taylor, Cameron, and Madison can be borne by male or female. This means that it is harder for prospective employers to tell a job applicant's sex when reading a résumé, a possible reason for the choices."

• **Spelling**. In his poem "Don Juan," Lord Byron wrote, "Thrice happy he whose name has been well spelt." Saddling your offspring with a weirdly spelled moniker like Chelsee, Geoffrey, or Jenifer means that the child will rack up hours of his or her life explaining to others how his or her name is spelled.

- **Initials**. Pay attention to the initials of your baby's name if they spell a word. It can be embarrassing and irritating to have the initials for Zackary Ian Thompson or Peter Ira Green or Donald Underwood Davis or Alice Samantha Sanders or Hannah Ann Gardner stamped on your jewelry, backpack, luggage, or psyche. A real-life initials trap turned out to be Ian Paul Daily (I. P. Daily). Make a final check to be sure that your baby's name does not create an unfortunate acronym. To avoid such crimson-faced accidents, spell a cheerful or neutral word, or none at all.

- **Length**. You can save your child a world of frustration when, later in life, he or she is filling out forms and applications by going easy on the syllables, especially if your last name is already long or complicated. The rule of thumb and naming is to confer a short first name upon a baby with a long last name and a longer first name to accompany a short last name.

- **Originality**. If you have a common surname like Smith, you would be wise to consider giving your bundle of joy a distinctive first and middle name. But a name that is bizarre may be a disservice to your child. A child with a popular name is likely to be more readily accepted by peers than a child with a weirdly uncommon name. You'll find out more when you read the coming chapter "Cruel and Unusual Names."

On his last day in Congress, Newt Gingrich appeared as a guest on the Tonight Show. The outgoing Speaker of the House told host Jay Leno, "I'm grateful to the country that a guy like me with a weird name would be allowed to lead the country."

- **Nicknames**. Think twice about conferring a name that is usually considered to be a nickname. That might be cute for a child but embarrassing and cloying after childhood. Billy works for a baby, but Billy will likely become Bill as a teenager and William as an adult professional. Bertie, Becky, Missy, Robby, and Weezy will have to spend hours of their lives explaining that they are not Albert, Rebecca, Melissa, Robert, and Louisa. Give your precious little ones names that age well. That would be traditional forms of their names so that they can choose the nicknames that will come and go with time.

> Father calls me William, sister calls me Will,
> Mother calls me Willie, but the fellows call me Bill!
> —Eugene Field

- **Religion**. If you wish to give your baby a name that honors your family's religion, the names of saints, heroes, and heroines with inspiring stories are plentiful. Little Anne, Christopher, David, Emily, Maria, and Mohamed will thank you one day.

• **Sound**. Keep your ears wide open for names that smoosh together. Think about the intersection between first and last names. In the playground, Stu Bass will be sure to be dubbed Stub Ass, Thomas Sweeney Thomas Weenie, and Mike Easter My Keister. I've met a fellow named Benjamin Nebola. Unfortunately, sounding both his names sounds like Benjamin Ebola, or Ben Ebola. Had his parents selected a first name that doesn't end in n, say Charles, that name, would have made it clear that his last name was Nebola, not Ebola.

• **Meanings**. Most names have meanings, so you should find out what your favorite choices for names mean before making them official. You'll find one-hundred-and-fifty first names and their meanings in the previous chapter and a myriad more in the mountain of baby name books on the market. Such diligence will ensure your children's happiness when one day they discover that their first name signifies a person who is noble, powerful, handsome, beautiful, admirable, or blessed and that you were so thoughtful in naming them.

• **Impressions**. Adolph used to be a fairly popular first name, as in film actor Adolphe Menjou and legendary basketball coach Adolph Rupp, but after the rise and fall of Adolf Hitler, Adolf and Adolph as birth names were vaporized. More recently, after the double whammy of a sex scandal and a catastrophic hurricane, Harvey has plummeted out of favor. Pressing into service an olfactory metaphor, Adolph and Harvey have been skunked.

Names telegraph messages about a person's family, ethnicity, gender, creativity, intelligence, and social standing. A name creates the first impression that other people gain about a person, especially if they read or hear that person's name before meeting them. A number of extensive surveys have queried people about the emotions engendered by certain names. When they are asked to stereotype names by age, attractiveness, competence, popularity, femininity/masculinity, and physical attributes, the respondents do tend to agree on each name's traits. You may wish to examine this research.

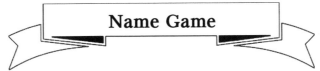

Name Game

Consider the twenty first names that follow. According to a recent baby name personality survey, which five boys' names communicate a first impression of intelligence and which five a first impression of not-so-smart? Then analyze the ten girls' names in the same manner.

boys: Abner, Alexander, David, Elmer, Emmett, Jethro, Jock, Samuel, Sebastian, Wendell

girls: Abigail, Bambi, Barbara, Bunny, Diana, Frederica, Honey, Kiki, Rebecca, Vanna

Answers

(according to The Sinrod Marketing Group Survey)

smart boys: Alexander, David, Samuel, Sebastian, Wendell

not-so-smart boys: Abner, Elmer, Emmett, Jethro, Jock

smart girls: Abigail, Barbara, Diana, Fredericka, Rebecca

not-so-smart girls: Bambi, Bunny, Honey, Kiki, Vanna

• **The "Junior" trap.** I can't describe this tender trap nearly as adroitly as the mother who wrote this letter:

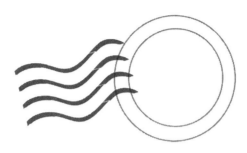

Dear Abby:

Please print my letter so other mothers won't make the same mistake I did. After 19 years, I realize the error of naming our son after his father.

When he was a boy, it was no problem. We called him Billy and his father was Bill.

When he got older, he decided that Billy was too babyish, so he asked us to call him Bill, which wasn't too bad. We called one Big Bill and the other Little Bill. That worked out fine until Little Bill got bigger than Big Bill.

Now it's worse. It's Young Bill and Old Bill, and you can imagine how thrilled father is to be Old Bill at 44. Not only that, but their voices are identical, and they are constantly being mistaken for one another on the telephone. And their mail gets mixed up, too.

It's a pain in the neck. I should have named him Lawrence, like I wanted to. I've always loved that name. Phooey on these Juniors.
—Too Late Now

Dear Too:

Thanks. New mothers, take note.

The Last Word
on Last Names

John Longfellow & Timothy Small

Names are powerful things.
They act as an identity marker and a kind of map,
locating you in time and geography.
More than that, they can be a compass.
—NICOLA YOON

Once you have a name, you have the beginning of understanding,
and once you have understanding, you lose fear.
God didn't want man to be fearful. He wanted man to be brave.
—JOHN KRAMER

Action without a name, a "who" attached to it, is meaningless.
—HANNAH ARENDT

I don't care what you say about me,
as long as you say something about me,
and as long as you spell my name right.
—GEORGE M. COHAN

The pattern of naming in the English language began with single names because, when people lived together in small communities, the supply of names was large enough that none had to be repeated in the same group. As social groups grew larger, the same single names began popping up more often, and a system of distinguishing among people with the same first names had to be invented. Thus, villagers began to add a bit of descriptive information to the given name, and that's how we got last names, or surnames. The *sur* in the word derives from the Latin *super* and means "above and beyond."

Some of these surnames began life as descriptions of a person's size—Small, Short, Little, Long, Longfellow, Stout; geography—Woods, Meadows, Burchfield, Churchill, Heath, Fields, Lane, Rivers, Brooks, Dale, Marsh, Grove, Newton (New Town),York, Lancaster, Kent; or personal qualities—Smart, Sharp, Wise, Swift, Young, Wild. One who refused to consume alcohol might have picked up the name Drinkwater, a man of great strength Armstrong, a lame man Cruikshank (crooked leg), a tough man Hardy, a happy-go-lucky man Blythe, and an exemplary person or loyal friend Truman, Goode, Goodman, Goodfellow, or Thoroughgood.

Another cluster of last names describes a person's hair or skin coloring: Black, Brown, Dunn, White. Variations of Red as a surname include

Reid, Reed, Read, Redd, Reddick, Redding, and Russell and the compounds Redbrook, Redfern, Redfield, Redford, Redgrave, Redman, Redmond, Redpath, and Redwood.

Other names are patronymics and matronymics (*patro* meaning "father,"*matro* meaning "mother," and *nym* meaning "name"), family names derived from a parent or ancestor. Your name is probably a patronymic if it begins with Mc (McDonald), Mac (MacLeod), O' (O'Brien), or Fitz (Fitzgerald), all of which mean "son of," or ends with son, sohn, sen, enko, ski, sky, off, ov, ove, ovich, wicz, or zn.

Just from the name John and its variations, we derive the patronymics Jones, Johnson, Johns, Evans, d'Giovanni, Hanson, Ibañez, Ivanov, Ivanovich, Jackson, Jantzen, Dujean, Lajean, Jenkins, Jensen, Jennings, Johansen, Juarez; O'Sean, and McShane.

Many Americans believe that the patronymic prefix Mc identifies Irish people and that Mac earmarks Scots. Au contraire. Mc is simply an abbreviation of Mac, and both Mc and Mac may signify either nationality, a claim that is proved by this traditional ditty:

> By Mac and O'
> You'll always know
> True Irishmen they say;
> For if they lack
> Both O' and Mac,
> No Irishmen are they.

The most extensive category of surnames began as descriptions of the work people did. In the telephone data bases of the world's English-speaking cities, Smith, which means "worker," is the most popular last name by a large margin over its nearest competitors—Johnson, Williams, Brown, Jones, Miller, Davis, Martin, Anderson, and Wilson. And it is no wonder when you consider that the village smith, who made and repaired most objects of metal, was among the most important persons in the community. Often Smith is compounded to indicate a greater degree of specialization, as in Arrowsmith, Coppersmith, Goldsmith, and Silversmith.

International variations on Smith include Smythe, Schmidt, Smed, Smitt, Faber, Faure, Ferraro, Ferrer, Ferrier, Ferron, Goff, Gough, Kovacs, Kovar, LeFebre, LeFevre, and Manx. Versions of Tailor/Taylor include Hiatt, Kravitz, Portnoy, Sarto, Sastre, Schneider, Snyder, Szabo, and Terzl. And Carpenters in other countries include Charpentier, Marangoz, Narangoz, Snedeker, Timmerman, and Zimmermann.

Some descriptive and occupational surnames were preceded by a *the* or *of the,* as in John the Smith or James of the Hill. These bridge words are usually omitted in Modern English, but they remain in some other languages. For example, De la Mare means "of the sea" and De Gaulle "of France."

It is easy to trace the occupational origins of names such as Abbott, Archer, Barber, Bowman, Butler, Carpenter, Carver, Cook, Draper, Farmer, Fisher, Forester, Fowler, Gardener, Glover, Hunter, Knight, Mason, Merchant, Miller, Naylor, Parsons, Piper, Potter, Priest, Saddler, Shoemaker, Sheppard, Shipman, Skinner, Spicer, Tanner, Taylor, Weaver, and Wheeler. Other surnames are not so easily recognized but yield up their occupational origins with some thought and research.

If your surname is Coleman or Collier, you have a forebear who mined coal. If your surname is Cooper, you have an ancestor who made barrels, if Hooper, your forefather made hoops for those barrels. William Shakespeare very likely had a progenitor who was a spear-shaker, that is, a soldier.

Webber means "a man who weaves," Webster "a woman who weaves." Brewer signifies "a man who brews," Brewster "a woman who brews." Dyer is the last name of "a man who dyes cloth," Dexter the last name of "a woman who dyes cloth." Baker, of course, denotes "a man who bakes," while Baxter denotes "a woman who bakes."

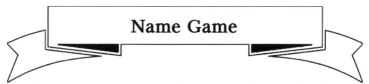

Name Game

In the following game, match each last name listed in the left-hand column with the corresponding trade in the right-hand column:

1.	Bailey	arrow maker
2.	Chandler	bailiff
3.	Clark	bargeman
4.	Cohen	candle maker
5.	Crocker	carpenter
6.	Faulkner	clerk
7.	Fletcher	dispenser of provisions
8.	Inman	doorkeeper
9.	Keeler	falconer

10.	Lardner	gamekeeper
11.	Lederer	innkeeper
12.	Marshall	keeper of horses
13.	Mercer	keeper of the cupboard
14.	Parker	leather worker
15.	Porter	merchant
16.	Sawyer	potter
17.	Schumacher	priest
18.	Scully	roofer
19.	Sherman	shearsman
20.	Spencer	scholar
21.	Stewart	shoemaker
22.	Thatcher	sty warden
23.	Travers	tile maker
24.	Tyler	toll-bridge collector
25.	Wainwright	wheel maker

Answers

1. bailiff 2. candle maker 3. clerk 4. priest 5. potter

6. falconer 7. arrow maker 8. innkeeper 9. bargeman 10. keeper of the cupboard

11. leather worker 12. keeper of horses 13. merchant 14. gamekeeper 15. doorkeeper

16. carpenter 17. shoemaker 18. scholar 19. shearsman 20. dispenser of provisions

21. sty warden 22. roofer 23. toll-bridge collector 24. tile maker 25. wheel maker

Keep in mind that the origins of some surnames are subject to various interpretations. For example, if your last name is Bell, your ancestor may have been a bell ringer or may have lived near the Bell Tavern or may simply have been smashingly good looking (*belle*).

In many cultures, when a woman marries, she relinquishes her last name and acquires that of her husband. Nowadays an increasing number of women have chosen to retain their surname. My wife, Simone van Egeren, is one of them. Feminist Gloria Steinem explains. "Many more women are keeping their birth names and not calling them maiden names, with all the sexual double standard that implies." Pakistani Prime Minister Benazir Bhutto put it this way: "Benazir Bhutto doesn't cease to exist the moment she gets married. I am not giving myself away. I belong to myself, and I always shall."

A striking characteristic of Spanish names, both in Spain and Hispanic America, is keeping the family name of the mother (*apellido materno* or *segundo apellido*), after the father's last name (*apellido paterno* or *primer apellido*). For example, Juan Acosta Lopez is the son of a father with the surname Acosta and a mother with the surname Lopez. Hispanics in the United States often drop their mothers' surnames.

African Americans abducted to America as slaves were often not allowed to keep their own Central or West African names. When a slave was sold, the new owner conferred a different first name upon his human property.

After Emancipation, many blacks chose surnames that expressed their freedom. They often adopted the last name of a white family, a benefactor, or a famous person whom they admired, such as Washington, Franklin, Jefferson, Jackson, or Douglas.

Recently, some African American Muslims have thrown off names that they perceive as shackles of slavery and embraced names of Islamic origin. For three famous examples, basketball great Lew Alcindor, boxer Cassius Marcellus Clay Jr., and playwright LeRoi Jones became, respectively Kareem Abdul-Jabbar, Amiri Baraka, and Muhammad Ali, who wrote, "Cassius Clay is a name that white people gave to my slave master. Now that I am free, that I don't belong to anyone anymore, I gave back that white name, and I chose a beautiful African one."

African Americans have also expressed a rich creativity in choosing first names that radiate style, attractiveness, and black identity. As David Zax has written in the online *Salon*, "The vast majority of unusual black names are like the catchy Maneesha and Tavonda, the magisterial Orencio and Percelle, or the evocative Lakazia and Swanzetta. They are names emerging from a tradition of linguistic and musical invention much like those that gave us jazz and rap. And they are names that have paved the way for Americans of all classes and colors to begin to loosen up the stodgy culture of traditional name giving. The census data show that whites, too, are increasingly looking for distinctive names."

For example, LaVar and Tina Ball (he's black and she's white), parents of three basketball-playing phenoms, named their sons Lonzo, LiAngelo, and LaMelo. For another example, in California more than 40 percent of African American girls are given first names that weren't bestowed on a single white girl in the state.

A Nickelodeon
of Nicknames

Nicknames are bestowed on members of a group by each other,
and only used within the group. At their core, group nicknames
are boundary-defining and boundary-maintaining mechanisms
that draw a line both between who is in a group of men
and who is out, and between that group and the outside world.
—BRETT AND KATY MCKAY

Nicknames stick to people,
and the most ridiculous are the most adhesive.
—THOMAS CHANDLER HALIBURTON

My parents actually named me Amelia,
but my sister took one look at me in the hospital and said, 'Minnie.'
Thanks a lot—my whole future was determined by a two-year-old.
—MINNIE DRIVER

A nickname is a substitution of a given name or surname for the purposes of affection, ridicule, or group identity. Most people acquire one or more nicknames during their lifetime; in fact, it's difficult to imagine someone who goes through life without a nickname. I, Richard Lederer, at various times in my life have been dubbed Richie, Rich, Dick, Rick, Link (from Link-Lederer, a play on the name of celebrity Art Linkletter), Super Cool, Jumbo (I'm kind of big), and Richard the Terd.

That nicknames are important to humans is shown by the many other words that mean the same thing—*affectionate name, appellation, by-name, cognomen, diminutive, epithet, familiar name, handle, moniker, pet name, sobriquet, tag,* and *term of endearment,* among other words. The key trait of nicknames is that they are bestowed upon a person by others. Some we acquire from those who love us, some from those who don't. A venerable piece of folk wisdom tells us that "a nickname is the hardest stone that the devil can throw at a man."

The word *nickname* boasts an ancient history. It first appeared in the 1300s in the English language as "an eke name," *eke* related to "augment" and meaning "also, additional." In the early 1500s, someone divided the words in the wrong way, and "an eke name" became "a nekename." From there it was only a short leap to "nickname." The spelling and meaning have stayed the same ever since. (A similar fate befell *a napron* and *a nuncle.*)

We can classify the content of nicknames into a number of categories:

• **physical characteristics**: Fatso, Pudge, Slim, Beanpole, Stretch, Long John, Shorty, Cutie, Curly, Baldy, Chrome Dome, Cue Ball, Pizza Face, Lefty, Schnoz, Gimpy, Shaky, Spaz;

• **coloring**: Blondie, Red, Pinky, Chalky, Blackie;

• **mental characteristics**: Genius, Einstein, Encyclopedia, Braniac, Sherlock, Noodlehead, Dopey;

• **personality**: Happy, Grumpy, Sleepy, Dizzy, Nerd, Badass, Motor Mouth, Chatterbox, Nervous Nellie, Sad Sack, Debbie Downer, Dork;

• **place of origin**: Boston, Dutch, Frenchy, Irish, Newfie, Tex;

• **accessories**: Four-Eyes, Metal Mouth, Train Tracks, Tin Teeth.

Most nicknames are shortenings of a proper name:

• **deleting the ending**: Chris from Christopher or Christine, Dave from David, Fran from Francis or Frances, Rich from Richard, Walt from Walter.

• **deleting the beginning**: Belle from Isabelle, Beth from Elizabeth, Drew from Andrew, Liam from William, Xander from Alexander.

• **deleting the beginning and the ending**: Liz from Elizabeth, Tori from Victoria, Trish from Patricia. Note that these names are all female. This kind of double clipping rarely happens to males, but note Gus from Augustus and Lex from Alexander.

• **adding the diminutive suffix ie, i,** or **y**: Alli, Annie, Bibi, Billy, Charlie, Franny, Suzie, Smitty.

• **reduplication (repetition of the same syllable)**: Bobo, Cici, Coco, Deedy, Fifi, Gigi, Jojo, Mimi. Most reduplicative names are female.

• **patronymic prefixes**: Fitz for Fitzgerald, Mac for McCarthy.

• **initials**: AJ for Anthony John, GBS for George Bernard Shaw, k.d. for Katherine Dawn Lang, O for Oprah Winfrey, Dubya for George W. Bush.

• **letter swapping**: From the Middle Ages on, initial letters in first names have been switched. Often the replacing first letter has been relocated forward to the lips or to the teeth because hard consonants are easier to pronounce than soft consonants. They fly from the front of the mouth like a watermelon seed. You can see this pattern at work in the evolution of Bob from Robert, Dick from Richard, Bill from William, Ted and Ned from Edward, Peg from Meg from Margaret, and Polly from Molly from Mary. The theory also works for the middle or end of a nickname, as in

Chip from Charles, Hal from Harold, Bart from Bartholomew, Rick from Richard, Libby from Elizabeth, and Sadie from Sarah.

• "kin"-ship: Before the seventeenth century, many nicknames included the endearing ending -in or -kin, where the ending was attached to the first syllable, as in Watkin for Walter, Thompkin for Thomas, and Simpkin for Simon. While most of these have died away, a few remain, such as Robin from Robert, Hank (Henkin) from Henry, Jack (Jankin) from John, and Colin (from Nicolas).

Nicknames can be monikers that people say to your face or those that they say behind your back. Do you suppose that even their best friends ever called President Richard Nixon "Tricky Dick" or President Bill Clinton "Slick Willy" or President Ulysses S. Grant "Useless Grant" to their faces? No way. "The Boss," "The Comeback Kid," and "Unconditional Surrender"? No problem.

In the world of entertainment, it's not unusual for famous people to be better known by their nicknames than their birth names. Rock bassist Gordon Matthew Thomas Sumner wore a yellow and black striped sweater when he played with the Phoenix Jazzmen during college vacations. They thought he looked like a wasp. You know him today as Sting.

Bono was born Paul David Hewson. The rock guitarist and singer received a series of nicknames as a teen and finally settled on Bono Vox, Latin for "good voice." It was later shortened to Bono.

Bruce Springsteen is nicknamed the Boss, Frank Sinatra Old Blue Eyes, Elvis Presley the King of Rock and Roll, Michael Jackson the King of Pop, Aretha Franklin the Queen of Pop, Jenny Lind the Swedish Nightingale, and John Wayne the Duke. Singer-parodist Al Yankovic's name is usually preceded by "Weird."

There is even a category called "Jazz Royalty." Think Duke Ellington; Count Basie; Nat King Cole; Ella Fitzgerald, The Queen of Jazz; Bessie Smith, The Empress of the Blues; Oscar Peterson, The Maharaja; Charles Mingus, The Baron; and Billie Holiday, Lady Day. Closely related are those who acquired "Jazz Divinity": Thelonious Monk, The High Priest of Soul; Nina Simone, the High Priestess of Soul; and Sarah Vaughn, the Divine One.

Opera sopranos Beverly Sills and Maria Callas were respectively nicknamed Bubbles and La Divina, while Old West entertainers and husband and wife William Frederick Cody and Annie Oakley took on the sobriquets Buffalo Bill and Little Miss Sure Shot.

Turning to history, it was at the First Battle of Bull Run, during the

American Civil War, that General Thomas Jackson acquired his enduring nickname. As his brigade stood firm in the face of a Union onslaught, General Barnard Bee exhorted his troops with "There is Jackson standing like a stone wall! Let us determine to die here, and we will conquer!" That's how Thomas Jackson became Stonewall Jackson. Shortly after shouting his famous rallying call, General Bee was mortally wounded.

Diminutive Stephen Douglas, best known for his stirring debates against Abraham Lincoln, was oxymoronically dubbed The Little Giant.

President Donald Trump has shown a flair for tarring his adversaries with sobriquets such as Crooked Hillary, Lyin' Ted, Little Marco, and Little Rocket Man.

When French President Charles de Gaulle was a young cadet in the military academy, he earned the nickname The Great Asparagus, conferred by his fellow cadets, who found his prodigious height and bulbous nose comical. Focusing on the general's nose, others dubbed him Cyrano, referring to the prodigious proboscis of Edmond Rostand's character Cyrano de Bergerac.

The Romans nicknamed Emperor Tiberius Nero because of his excessive drinking. They dubbed him Biberius Mero, "a Mere Imbiber," *mere* meaning that the wine that he unstintingly imbibed was undiluted). Another Roman emperor, Caligula ("little soldier's boot"), was actually named Gaius Julius Caesar Augustus Germanicus.

Italian Renaissance painter Alessandro di Mariano di Vanni Filipepi is better known to us as Sandro Botticelli. He received the nickname from his brother, who himself evidently resembled a *botticello* or "little barrel." Tintoretto, born Jacopo Comin, was also called Il Furioso for the energy shown in his paintings. His father was a dyer, *tintore*, so his son was called "little dyer."

Mass murderers acquire nicknames like The Night Stalker, The Unabomber, Jack the Ripper, and The Boston Strangler.

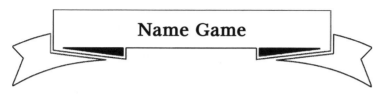

Name Game

Match each nickname with each original name:

1. The Bard of Avon	Al Capone
2. The Belle of Amherst	Charles Lindberg
3. Billy the Kid	Elizabeth I
4. Bloody Mary	Emily Dickinson
5. The British Bulldog	Erwin Rommel
6. The Desert Fox	Florence Nightingale
7. Evita	Geoffrey Chaucer
8. The Father of English Literature	George Patton
9. The Greatest Showman on Earth	Henry McCarty
10. The Iron Lady	Joan of Arc
11. The Lady with the Lamp	Manfred von Richthofen
12. Lionheart	Margaret Thatcher
13. The Little Corporal	María Eva Duarte de Perón
14. Lucky Lindy	Mary Tudor (Queen Mary I)
15. The Maid of Orléans	Napoleon Bonaparte
16. Old Blood and Guts	Phineas T. Barnum
17. The Red Baron	Richard I
18. Scarface	Thomas Edison
19. The Virgin Queen	William Shakespeare
20. The Wizard of Menlo Park	Winston Churchill

Answers

1. William Shakespeare. Some students have nicknamed the Bard "Willie Wigglestaff" ("Shake-Spear") 2. Emily Dickinson 3. Henry McCarty (aka William H. Bonney or Henry Antrim) 4. Mary Tudor (Queen Mary I) 5. Winston Churchill

6. Erwin Rommel 7. María Eva Duarte de Perón 8. Geoffrey Chaucer 9. Phineas T. Barnum 10. Margaret Thatcher

11. Florence Nightingale 12. Richard I 13. Napoleon Bonaparte 14. Charles Lindberg 15. Joan of Arc

16. George Patton 17. Manfred von Richthofen 18. Al Capone 19. Elizabeth I 20. Thomas Edison

An All-Star Lineup
of Nicknames

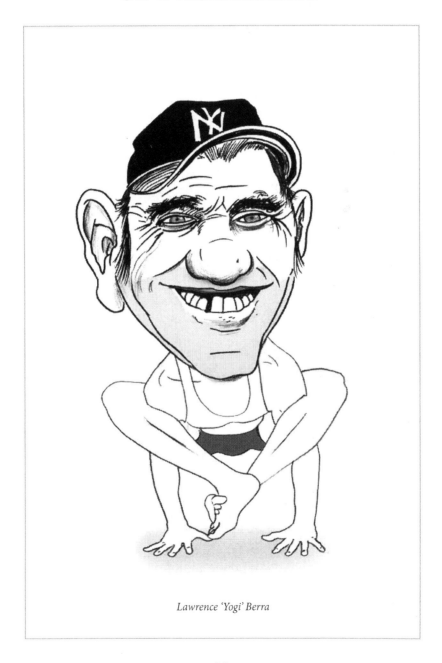

Lawrence 'Yogi' Berra

Most of us have nicknames—annoying, endearing, embarrassing.
But what about your true name?
It is not necessarily your given name.
But it is the one to which you are most eager to respond when called.
—VERA NAZARIAN

The world of sports sparks forth a gallery of sporty nicknames: Think of golfers Eldrick Tont "Tiger" Woods and Jack "The Golden Bear" Nicklaus; boxers Ray "Boom Boom" Mancini; Joe Louis, "The Brown Bomber"; "Sugar Ray" Robinson (and "Sugar Ray" Leonard); and Muhammad Ali, "The Greatest"; football players Harold Edward "Red" Grange, "The Galloping Ghost"; Bronislau "Bronco" Nagurski; Elroy "Crazylegs" Hirsch; William "The Refrigerator" Perry; Ed "Too Tall" Jones; Kenny "The Snake" Stabler' and, more recently, Rob Gronkowski, often dubbed "Gronk" and hockey legend Wayne "The Great" Gretzky (possibly inspired by F. Scott Fitzgerald's great novel *The Great Gatsby*).

Basketball superstar Wilt Chamberlain and I grew up in West Philadelphia at the same time. In those days a man seven feet tall, built like Superman, and possessed with preternatural skill in multiple sports was something new. As Wilt's Overbrook High School basketball team annually crushed our West Philly High School squad, he acquired the nicknames "Wilt the Stilt" and "The Big Dipper."

Basketball holds court to a gallery of colorful nicknames, as the following challenge will reveal:

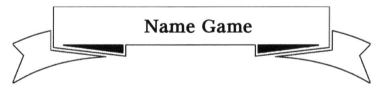

Name Game

Match each nickname with each basketball star's real name:

1.	Charles Barkley	The Admiral
2.	Larry Bird	The Answer
3.	Darryl Dawkins	Chocolate Thunder
4.	Clyde Drexler	Doctor Dunkenstein
5.	Julius Erving	Doctor J
6.	George Gervin	The Dream

7.	Darrell Griffith	The Glide
8.	Anfernee Hardaway	His Airness
9.	Allen Iverson	The Human Highlight Reel
10.	LeBron James	The Iceman
11.	Earvin Johnson	King James
12.	Michael Jordan	Larry Legend
13.	Karl Malone	Magic
14.	Pete Maravich	The Mailman
15.	Earl Monroe	Mister Clutch
16.	Hakeem Olajuwon	The Pearl
17.	David Robinson	Penny
18.	Dennis Rodman	Pistol Pete
19.	Jerry West	The Round Mound of Rebound
20.	Dominique Wilkens	The Worm

Answers

1. The Round Mound of Rebound 2. Larry Legend 3. Chocolate Thunder 4. The Glide 5. Doctor J

6. The Iceman 7. Doctor Dunkenstein 8. Penny 9. The Answer 10. King James

11. Magic 12. His Airness 13. the Mail Man 14. Pistol Pete 15. The Pearl

16. the Dream 17. the Admiral 18. the Worm 19. Mr. Clutch (also Zeke from Cabin Creek) 20. the Human Highlight Reel

But it is the great American game of baseball that has bequeathed us the widest world of nicknames:

At the start of the 1976 baseball season, the Detroit Tigers unveiled Mark "The Bird" Fidrych, one of the most exciting rookie pitchers in the history of baseball. In his autobiography No Big Deal, Fidrych reveals how his avian nickname was conferred on him by one of his coaches, Jeff Hogan. "I just run out on the field and he goes, 'Bird.' And I just turn around. And he goes, 'That's your nickname I gave you.' And I said, 'What did you call me that for?' And he said, 'You look like that goofy bird in Sesame Street. Fidrych is too hard to, y'know, say."

In his first year, Fidrych won nineteen games and lost nine, accumulating a league-leading ERA of 2.34 and was voted American League Rookie of the year. Sadly, the pitcher, plagued by knee and shoulder problems, never lived up to his early promise, but for a few years he was the most famous Bird until a fellow named Larry Bird changed what it meant to play the game of basketball.

Many of us fondly recall bygone days when baseball players were anointed with colorful nicknames. Ted Williams, for example, was variously dubbed "The Splendid Splinter," "The Kid," "Teddy Ballgame," and "The Thumper." Similarly, George Herman Ruth took on the monikers "Babe," "The Bambino," and "The Sultan of Swat" and Joe DiMaggio "The Yankee Clipper" and "Joltin' Joe."

Where have all the baseball nicknames gone? Long time passing. Where have all the nicknames gone? Long time ago. The way-back machine brings us colorful characters such as Walter "Big Train" Johnson, Lou "The Iron Horse" Gehrig, Pete "Charlie Hustle" Rose, Ernie "Mr. Cub" Banks, and "Hammerin'" Hank Aaron (and "Hammerin'" Hank Greenburg). More recently, we watched the play of Frank "The Big Hurt" Thomas, Randy "the Big Unit" Johnson, Alex "A-Rod" Rodriguez, and David "Big Papi" Ortiz.

Today? Can you name any baseballers with beguiling nicknames? Maybe, but just a few. The art of the classic cognomen seems to have gone the way of fountain pens, phonographs, typewriters, and telephone booths.

ESPN announcer and analyst Chris "Boomer" Berman made it his mission to confer punderful nicknames on hundreds of athletes—Sammy "Say It Ain't" Sosa, Bert "I'll be Home" Blyleven, Ryan Bowen "Arrow," Mike "Pepperoni" Piazza, Bruce "Eggs" Benedict, and Bruce Bochy "Ball," among them.

"I viewed it as a lost art," Berman explained. "Why aren't there nicknames now? Maybe everything is so literal. You can see everybody on the internet, TV, YouTube, whatever it is. There's very little left to the imagination."

Magazine editors and writers Brett and Kate McKay confirm and extend Berman's theory: "Today's athletes lack the intimacy and accessibility that allowed nicknames to thrive, and because all nicknames are bestowed by others and thus lie outside the control of the named, modern athletes often eschew them in favor of stricter management of their personal brand."

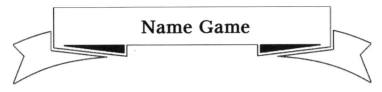

Name Game

Play ball, sports junkies, word buffs, old-timers, and young-timers! Match each baseball all-star with his nickname:

1.	John Baker	The Barber
2.	Lawrence Berra	Big Poison
3.	Dennis Boyd	Blue Moon
4.	Mordecai Brown	Bucky
5.	Roger Clemens	Casey
6.	Clarence Coleman	Catfish
7.	Ty Cobb	Choo-Choo
8.	Jay Dean	Country
9.	Paul Dean	Cy
10.	Russell Dent	Daffy
11.	Leo Durocher	Dizzy
12.	Bob Feller	Doctor K
13.	Carlton Fisk	Ducky
14.	Frankie Frisch	Duke
15.	Dwight Gooden	The Flying Dutchman
16.	Rich Gossage	The Fordham Flash
17.	Robert Green	Gabby
18.	Robert Grove	The Georgia Peach
19.	Ken Harrelson	Goose
20.	Charles Hartnett	The Hat
21.	Rogers Hornsby	Hawk
22.	Jim Hunter	Home Run
23.	Joe Jackson	Killer
24.	Reggie Jackson	Klu
25.	William Keeler	King Kong
26.	Harmon Killebrew	Lefty
27.	Dave Kingman	The Lip
28.	Ted Kluszewski	The Man
29.	Bill Lee	Mr. October
30.	Salvatore Maglie	Oil Can
31.	Walter Maranville	Pee Wee

32.	Willie Mays	Pie
33.	Joe Medwick	Pudge
34.	Stan Musial	Pumpsie
35.	John Odom	Rabbit
36.	Leroy Paige	The Rajah
37.	Harold Reese	Rapid Robert
38.	Phil Rizzuto	Red
39.	Albert Schoendienst	The Rocket
40.	Enos Slaughter	Satchel
41.	Ozzie Smith	Say Hey
42.	Edwin Snider	Scooter
43.	Charles Stengel	Shoeless Joe
44.	Harold Traynor	Spaceman
45.	Honus Wagner	Three Finger
46.	Harry Walker	Wee Willie
47.	Paul Waner	Wild Thing
48.	Mitch Williams	The Wizard of Oz
49.	Yastrzemski	Yaz
50.	Denton Young	Yogi

Answers

1. Home Run 2. Yogi 3. Oil Can 4. Three Finger 5. The Rocket 6. Choo-Choo 7. The Georgia Peach 8. Dizzy 9. Daffy 10. Bucky

11. The Lip 12. Rapid Robert 13. Pudge (also Ivan Rodriguez) 14. The Fordham Flash 15. Doctor K 16. Goose 17. Pumpsie 18. Lefty 19. Hawk 20. Gabby

21. The Rajah 22. Catfish 23. Shoeless Joe 24. Mr. October 25. Wee Willie (also Hit 'Em Where They Ain't) 26. Killer 27. King Kong 28. Klu 29. Spaceman 30. The Barber

31. Rabbit 32. Say Hey 33. Ducky 34. The Man 35. Blue Moon 36. Satchel; 37. Pee Wee 38. Scooter 39. Red (also Charles Ruffing) 40. Country

41. The Wizard of Oz 42. Duke 43. Casey 44. Pie 45. The Flying Dutchman 46. The Hat 47. Big Poison 48. Wild Thing 49. Yaz 50. Cy

Cruel and Unusual Names

Hedda Lettuce

The great William Shakespeare said, "What's in a name?" He also said,
"Call me Billy one more time and I will stab you with this ink quill."
— CUTHBERT SOUP

In William Shakespeare's *Romeo and Juliet*, the young heroine utters the immortal lines

> *What's in a name? That which we call a rose*
> *By any other name would smell as sweet.*

By the end of the play we know that Juliet was wrong. That her name is Capulet and Romeo's Montague leads to the deaths of the two young lovers.

What's in a name? A great deal, as anyone who has ever been stuck with a cruel name or nickname will tell you. Would a rose by any other name really smell as sweet? Many believe that a rose by another name might smell like a petunia, or a stinkweed. The children's chant "Sticks and stones can break my bones, but names can never hurt me" is a whistle in the dark to ward off the centuries-old belief that names can indeed hurt us.

Children are legally protected from physical cruelty by their parents. Why shouldn't they be protected against the mental cruelty of a thoughtlessly conferred name? Insightful Groucho Marx once observed, "Some day there will have to be some new rules established about name-calling. I don't mean the routine cursing that goes on between husband and wife, but the naming of defenseless, unsuspecting babies."

The most notorious example of Groucho's interdiction is Ima Hogg, the daughter of James Stephen "Big Jim" Hogg, a late-nineteenth-century attorney general and governor of Texas. As if her albatross name wasn't enough of a burden, Ima Hogg had to deal with unstinting rumors that she had sisters stuck with the names Ura Hogg and Wera Hogg. That's fake news. Ima had only brothers.

Then there were the hypochondriacal Jacksons, who named their six children Appendicitis, Jakeitis, Laryngitis, Meningitis, Peritonitis, and Tonsillitis.

Less guilty is the foreign couple who decided to name their first daughter with the most beautiful English word they had ever heard. They named her Diarrhea.

Groucho may be right. A great number of countries, including France, Hungary, and New Zealand, have laws that require parents to name their babies from a pre-approved registry and bar the bestowing of ridiculous and shameful names. But such is not the case in the Unites States. Here's a parade of funny, whimsical, strange, and unfortunate names arranged by category:

• *prehistoric creatures*: Jurassic Park, Terryl Dactyl, Dina Soares, Tyrannosaurus Rex;

• *animals*: Allie Katt, Peter Rabbitt, Katz Meow, Bopeep Seahorse, Bear Trapp, Burpee Fox, Preserved Fish, Uncas Peacock, Earl E. Bird, Toxen Worm;

• *objects*: Carr Chase, Iona Carr, Formica Dinette, Alma Knack, Ray Gunn, Canon Ball, Sherman Tank, Fanny Pack, Clara Net, the brothers Majestic and Scientific Mapp, Holland Tunnell, Valentine Card, Birdie Greenhouse, Jim Shortz, Orphia Outhouse, Stanley Cupp, Yolanda Squatpump, Pearl E. Gates, Noah Zark;

• *botany*: Ivy Snow Frost, Pete Moss, Magnolia Flowers, Prickly Thorne, Pansy Flowers Greenwood, Rosy Geranium, Douglass Furr, Honeysuckle Ginsburg, Lily La Fleur;

• *nature*: April Showers, Rainbow Aurora, Cori Ander, Ode Mountain DeLorenzo Malone, Poppy Honey Rose Bush, Sparrow James Midnight Madden, Birdie Tinkle, Morning Dew, Nighten Day;

• *toys*: Barbie Dahl, Teddy Bear, Perley Marble, Marionette Wisdom, Gocart Bogard, Iwanna Batt;

The fame that engulfs celebrities sometimes compels them to "gift" their kids with names that are certain to be ridiculed later in schoolyards. Maybe the generator of this trend is that celebrities crave attention, so they bestow upon their progeny attention-grabbing monikers.

Magician Penn Jillette named his daughter Moxie Crimefighter. Kim Kardashian and Kanye West named their first daughter North, as in North West, their son Saint, and their second daughter Chicago. John Mellencamp bestowed upon his son the name Speck Wildhorse. Comedian and civil rights activist Dick Gregory coalesced his two callings by anointing his twins with the middle names Inte and Gration. Paula Yates and British rocker Bob Geldof named their four daughters Fifi Trixiebelle, Peaches, Pixie, and Heavenly Hirani Tiger Lily. And Frank Zappa and wife brought forth children named Diva Thin Muffin, Dweezil, and Moon Unit.

Add to the marquee of ridiculous celebrity baby names Poppy Honey, Daisy Boo, River Rocket, Petal Blossom Rainbow, Pilot Inspektor, Audio Science, Rocket Zot Worthington, Lyric Angel, God'Iss Love, Jermajesty, and Zuma Nesta Rock, and you have a community of babies who will one day spend many hours on a psychiatrist's couch.

Non-celebrities have contributed their share of equally freaky names, which include Althea Anna Tomic, Billion Ayer, Jed I. Knight, Paul Bearer, Mad Laughinghouse, Vaseline Heart, Hans Ohff, Sip Passwater, Philina Blank, Concepcion Love, Charles Faux-Pas Bidet, Laura Lynn Hardy, Wendy Wacko, I. Q. Smart, Safety First, Mona Lotty, Miscellany Marchbanks, Aurelian Schexnader, Drucilla Prabilla, Capers C. Funnye, Illtread Lecher, Iwanna Looney, Fritioff Q. Fryxell, Virtue Blaring, Urbin Bowels, and Rowdy Negro.

As a denouement, savor a feast of eye-catching, ear-rinsing monikers. The banquet begins with an appetizer of Dyl Pickle, Hedda Lettuce, and Olive Green, along with Anna Coolbroth. For the meat portion you can select Filet Minyon, Virginia Ham, Frank Hamburger, Frank Furter, Lotta Ham, Angus Pattie, Yolanda Bologna, Beatrix Meats Balls, Chris P. Bacon, or Pork Chop, accompanied by Tuna Fish, Frieda Egg, Mac Aroni, Oliver Onion, Mabel Green Bean, Brock Lee, Starlight Cauliflower Shaw, Lotta Parsley, Coal Slaw, Midriff Billy Toast, Ruby Strawberry, Kandi Apple, Ginger Snap, Melba Toast, or Mustard M. Mustard.

For dessert enjoy Orange Marmalade Lemon, Cherry Tarte, Apple Cobbler, Rosebud Custard, or Craven Tart and wash down the repast with Dr. Pepper, Thomas Cola, Marijuana Pepsi Jackson, Sally Shake, Hazel Nutt Coffee, or, more intoxicatingly, Bud Lite, Madonna Beers, Dom Perignon Champagne, or Lisa Redwine (who actually is a sommelier!).

Did you Etta Lot of that Al Dente Hearty Meal?

Fascinating Facts
About Names

Albert Einstein

The beginning of all wisdom is to call things by their right names.
　　—CHINESE PROVERB

With knowledge of the name
comes a distincter recognition of the thing.
　　—HENRY DAVID THOREAU

D o animals name other animals in their group? A recent study of Campbell's monkeys on Sierra Leone and Ivory Coast showed that monkey calls are far more sophisticated than previously thought, and the primates can even form basic "sentences" to communicate. Researchers found that the same species of monkeys located in separate geographic regions use their alarm calls differently to warn of approaching predators, distinguishing between eagles and leopards. Similar distinctions may have been a precursor to human naming by our ancient ancestors.

Two other recent inquiries, at the University of California Santa Cruz and Emory University, posit that elephant seals and cetaceans (whales, dolphins, and porpoises), which live in tightly knit, socially complex groups, appear to "converse." The studies note that individuals emit unique calls and whistles that may very well function as names for other individuals in the group.

***

We are used to the general pattern of first name-middle name-last name, called the western order, but many places in the world don't adhere to that sequence.

The Chinese normally have two names, a personal name and a surname, but the surname comes first, then the personal name. This is called the eastern order. Some Chinese reverse the order when they come to live in the west.

The custom of placing the family name first also appears in many countries where the Chinese were influential, such as Japan, Korea, Singapore, Taiwan, Vietnam, and parts of India. Surprisingly, the same custom is followed in parts of Austria, Bavaria, France, Belgium, Greece, Italy, Madagascar, and Sri Lanka, where there was little Chinese influence.

***

A country of seventeen thousand islands, Indonesia has more than three-hundred-and-fifty tribal or ethnic groups, all with different customs. Many Indonesians have single names. Others have more than one name, but nothing that we would call a last name. A third group uses the father or mother's name as a hereditary last name, as we do.

***

Muhammad (also spelled Mohammed and Mohammad) is the most popular first name in the world. Globally, the most common surnames are, in order, Lee (or Li), Zhang, Wang, Nguyen, Garcia, Gonzalez, Hernandez, Smith, Smirnov, and Müller.

***

A number of people possess a single letter for a surname, and you can't get shorter than that. Some of them are listed as I, and I nominate that as the shortest surname because it is the skinniest.

When I was a callow youth growing up in Philadelphia, one Adolph Blaine Charles David Earl Frederick Gerald Hubert Irvin John Kenneth Lloyd Martin Nero Oliver Paul Quincy Randolph Sherman Thomas Uncas Victor William Xerxes Yancy Zeus Wolfeschlegelsteinhausenbergerdorff, Senior, was listed in our telephone book and was considered to be the longest name in the world.

Years later, Mr. W expanded his name to:

Adolph Blaine Charles David Earl Frederick Gerald Hubert Irvin John Kenneth Lloyd Martin Nero Oliver Paul Quincy Randolph Sherman Thomas Uncas Victor William Xerxes Yancy Zeus Wolfe-schlegel-stein-hausen-berger-dorff-welche-vor-altern-waren-gewissen-haft-schafers-wessen-schafe-waren-wohl-gepflege-und-sorg-faltig-keit-be-schutzen-vor-an-greifen-durch-ihr-raub-gierig-feinde-welche-vor-altern-zwolf-hundert-tausend-jah-res-voran-die-er-scheinen-von-der-erste-erde-mensch-der-raum-schiff-genacht-mit-tung-stein-und-sieben-iridium-elek-trisch-mo-tors-ge-brauch-licht-als-sein-ur-sprung-von-kraft-ge-start-sein-lange-fahrt-hin-zwischen-stern-artig-raum-auf-der-suchen-nach-bar-schaft-der-stern-welche-ge-habt-be-wohn-bar-planeten-kreise-drehen-sich-und-wo-hin-der-neue-rasse-von-ver-stand-ig-mensch-lich-keit-konnte-fort-pflanzen-und-sicher-freuen-an-lebens-lang-lich-freude-und-ru-he-mit-nicht-ein-furcht-vor-an-greifen-vor-anderer-intelligent-ge-schopfs-von-hin-zwisch-en-stern-art-ig-raum, Senior.

Also known as Wolfe+585, Mr. W held the record for the longest personal name in history, from year 1975 until his death in 1985, with a whopping 746 letters. His hippopoyomonstrosesquipedalian surname was preceded by twenty-six names, each beginning with sequential letters of the alphabet. Here's an English translation of his surname:

A descendant of one who prepared wool for manufacture on a stone, living in a house in the mountain village, who before ages was a conscientious shepherd whose sheep were well tended and diligently protected against attackers who by their rapacity were enemies who 12,000 years ago appeared from the stars to the humans by spaceships with light as an origin of power, started a long voyage within starlike space in search for the star which has habitable planets orbiting and on which the new race of reasonable humanity could thrive and enjoy lifelong happiness and tranquility without fear of attack from other intelligent creatures from within starlike space.

Coming in second:

Red Wacky League Antlez Broke the Stereo Neon Tide Bring Back Honesty Coalition Feedback Hand of Aces Keep Going Captain Let's Pretend Lost State of Dance Paper Taxis Lunar Road Up Down Strange! All and I Neon Sheep Eve Hornby Faye Bradley AJ Wilde Michael Rice Dion Watts Matthew Appleyard John Ashurst Lauren Swales Zoe Angus Jaspreet Singh Emma Matthews Nicola Brown Leanne Pickering Victoria Davies Rachel Burnside Gil Parker Freya Watson Alisha Watts James Pearson Jacob Sotheran-Darley Beth Lowery Jasmine Hewitt Chloe Gibson Molly Farquhar Lewis Murphy Abbie Coulson Nick Davies Harvey Parker Kyran Williamson Michael Anderson Bethany Murray Sophie Hamilton Amy Wilkins Emma Simpson Liam Wales Jacob Bartram Alex Hooks Rebecca Miller Caitlin Miller Sean McCloskey Dominic Parker Abbey Sharpe Elena Larkin Rebecca Simpson Nick Dixon Abbie Farrelly Liam Grieves Casey Smith Liam Downing Ben Wignall Elizabeth Hann Danielle Walker Lauren Glen James Johnson Ben Ervine Kate Burton James Hudson Daniel Mayes Matthew Kitching Josh Bennett Evolution Dreams.

Yep, that's one person's full name. In fact, it's the longest name (160 words) of any living person because it includes the names of those helped by a charity called Red Dreams set up by one Dawn McManus in memory of her son. The British resident legally changed her name to the above to honor them.

***

The letter *J* begins more American and British first names than any other, and the letter *S* begins more American and British surnames than any other. *X* is the least common letter to kick off an English last name.

***

During the European Renaissance, the spelling of words and names was not fixed. As far as we can tell, William Shakespeare never signed his name as Shakespeare, the way we spell it today. Literary references to him during his lifetime and after he shuffled off this mortal coil include the renderings Shakespear, Shake-spear, Shak-speare Shakespere, Shakspear, Shakspeare, Shakesper, Shakspere, Shaxberd, Shaxpaire, and Shaxpere, as well as Shakespeare, the version that adorns the First Folio.

The story is the same with Shakespeare's contemporary Sir Walter Raleigh, the spelling that posterity has preferred. His contemporaries and successors wrote to or about him employing the spellings Ralegh, Rawleigh, Rawleighe, Raleghe, Rawlegh, Rawleigh, Rawlighe, Rawlye, Rawleygh, Raghley, Raghlie, Rauhleigh, Rawle, Rawley, Rawely, and Raweley, among other representations. Sir Walter changed the spelling of his surname throughout his life, but never spelled it Raleigh. His only known signature is Ralegh.

But the name of the long-time and late Libyan strongman may be the most multiply spelled of anyone's in history. We're talking about Colonel Gaddafi—or is it Gadafy or Gathafi or Kaddafi or Qaddafi or Qadhafi? Once you've selected a spelling of the last name you have to decide whether you want to add the Arabic prefix *al-*, which can also be rendered as *el-*. Then the question becomes whether that prefix should be capitalized or lowercased and hyphenated or unhyphenated.

Unsurprisingly, the transliteration of the international troublemaker's first name is equally troublesome. Is it spelled Moamar or Moammar or Muammar or Mu'ammar? ABC news, which publishes the name as Moammar Gaddafi, once posted a list of 112 variations of the Brother Leader's full name.

***

A chasm stretches between the spelling and actual pronunciation of some surnames, most notably Beauchamp: "Beecham," Cholomodeley: "Chumley," Mainwearing: "Mannering," and—ta da!—Featherstone-haugh: "Fanshaw"!

***

Social observer and comedian savant George Carlin gave us "Do you know why hurricanes have names instead of numbers? To keep the killing personal. No one cares about a bunch of people killed by a number. 200 DEAD AS NUMBER THREE SLAMS ASHORE is not nearly as interesting a headline as CHARLIE KILLS 200. Death is much more satisfying and entertaining if you personalize it."

In 1953 the National Weather Service began conferring female first names on all hurricanes. When I was a boy, we bandied about a little riddle: "Why do they give hurricanes female names?" "Because otherwise, they'd be himmicanes!" Har har.

Happily, that joke doesn't work anymore because in 1978, the Weather Service started alternating male and female names for these death-dealing, property-annihilating storms. That's one giant step for humankind. As the vice president of the National Organization for Women explained, "Women are not disasters, destroying life and community and leaving a lasting and devastating effect."

Turns out that when it comes to hurricanes, the female is deadlier than the male. Sexism isn't just a social disease; it can kill you. That's the conclusion of a team of researchers who published their findings in the *Proceedings of the National Academy of Sciences.* After reviewing death rates from hurricanes that wreaked havoc from 1950 to 2012, they concluded, "Feminine-named hurricanes (vs. masculine-named hurricanes) cause significantly more deaths, apparently because they lead to a lower perceived risk and consequently less preparedness." Duh!

***

A capitonym is a word that changes meaning and pronunciation when it is capitalized, as in "*Job* got a *job.*" Capitonyms that are human names include *Begin/begin, Breathed/breathed, Degas/degas, Dieter/dieter, Guy/guy, Herb/herb, Levy/levy, Millet/millet, Ram/ram,* and *Ravel/ravel.*

***

The name John can be transmuted phonetically into seven other names or nicknames simply by changing the internal vowel sound—Jan, Jane, Jean/Gene, Jen, Joan, and June.

***

Albert Einstein was the quintessential scientific iconoclast. An iconoclast is literally "a breaker of idols," and Einstein destroyed many of the venerated scientific beliefs of his day. He also smashed the "*i* before *e,* except after *c*" spelling rule, because his last name itself is a double violation.

***

Many names perform the double duty of being either a first name or last name. Examples include Aaron, Allison, Arnold, Aubrey, Avery, Clark, Craig, Dennis, Douglas, George, Gordon, Harvey, Henry, Howard, Jordan, Lester, Lloyd, Lowell, Madison, Martin, Page, Scott, Sheldon, Sidney, Taylor, Thomas, and Wallace. This phenomenon allows us to construct strings of names in which each dynamic duo is the name of a famous person: *Minnie Pearl Buck Henry James [Russell] Lowell Thomas Brady Anderson Cooper Manning.*

***

It's clear that alliteration, the repetition of initial consonant sounds, is the key to being a great home run hitter. Just look at the names of the three men who have smashed the most home runs in a single baseball season—Barry Bonds (73 homers), Mark McGuire (70), and Sammy Sosa (66).

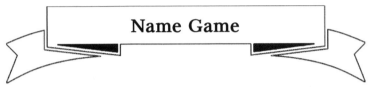

Name Game

Throughout history, the number three has held great power and fascination for humankind. We think about time as past, present, and future. We divide our days into morning, noon, and night; our meals into breakfast, lunch, and dinner; our government into executive, legislative, and judicial; the elements into solid, liquid, and gas; our world into land, sea, and air; humanity into man, woman, and child; the necessities into food, shelter, and clothing; gender into masculine, feminine, and neuter; our minds into id, ego, and superego and our primary colors into red, blue, and yellow.

The same is true with names, which are often grouped into dynamic trios. In the Bible, we read about the three patriarchs, Abraham, Isaac, and Jacob; the men who emerged from the fiery furnace, Shadrach, Meshach, and Abednego; and the three wise men, Gaspar, Melchior, and Balthasar, bearing gold, frankincense, and myrrh.

For the ancient Greeks, Zeus ruled the sky with his three-forked lightning bolt, Poseidon the sea with his trident, and Hades the underworld with Cerberus, his three-headed dog. In Hinduism the deities are Brahma the creator, Vishnu the preserver, and Shiva the destroyer.

Stop, look, and listen: Consider triads, triplets, triumvirates, and troikas of people who hang around together. For each of these *a, b,* and *c* dynamic trios I give you, alphabetically, the last item and ask you to supply the first two:

1. and Aramis 2. and Brahms 3. and Cordelia 4. and Cottontail 5. and Harry 6. and Jack 7. and Louie 8. and Mary 9. and Nash 10. and Nod

Answers

1. Porthos, Athos, 2. Bach, Beethoven, 3. Goneril, Regan, 4. Flopsy, Mopsy, 5. Tom, Dick,

6. Manny, Moe, 7. Huey, Dewey, 8. Peter, Paul, 9. Crosby, Stills, 10. Wynken, Blynken

Marquee Monikers

Julius Marx

At a time when studios created names and images to go with them,
"Meryl Streep" wouldn't have lasted ten minutes.
—GERALD NACHMAN

Pflug is a name you change from, not to.
—JO ANN PFLUG
(when asked if Pflug was her real name or a stage name)

The very first Academy Awards ceremony took place during a banquet held in the Blossom Room of the Hollywood Roosevelt Hotel. Two hundred and seventy attended, tickets cost ten dollars, and the awards part of the evening lasted fifteen minutes. When the first awards were handed out on May 16, 1929, movies had just begun to talk.

If you're a movie buff, you might be interested in the origin of the name for the gold-plated statuette awarded by the Academy of Motion Picture Arts and Sciences. The figurines were first conferred in 1929 but did not receive their nickname Oscar until 1931, when Margaret Herrick, executive librarian of the organization, exclaimed within earshot of newspaper reporter Sidney Skolsky that the statuette looked "just like my Uncle Oscar." Granting the statuette a name has enhanced the popular appeal of the entire awards ceremony.

Hollywood's star-makers capitalize on the fact that people react emotionally to names. A star's name must have "box-office appeal" and must project the kind of image that the star is supposed to radiate.

Would W. C. Fields have been as funny if he had retained his original name—William Claude Dukenfield—or Doris Day as popular if she had kept hers—Doris Mary Ann Kappelhoff? Would Marilyn Monroe have been as seductive if she had kept her name Norma Jean Mortensen? Would William Henry Pratt have been as scary if he hadn't undergone a name transplant and become Boris Karloff? And would the Marx Brothers have been as funny is they had not changed their names from Julius, Arthur, and Leonard to Groucho, Harpo, and Chico?

Turning to western stars, did Marion Michael Morrison's image become more macho when his studio changed his name to John Wayne? Would Roy Rogers have been such an iconic cowboy if he had kept his original moniker, Leonard Franklin Slye? And would Harold Preston Smith, a Mohawk Indian and grandson of a chief, have become the Lone Ranger's partner Tonto if he hadn't changed his name to Jay Silverheels?

The actor Stewart Granger was born James Stewart, but Jimmy Stewart had shot to fame before Granger's career, so the other James Stewart had to alter his name to Stewart Granger. Comic Albert Brooks changed his name because he was born Albert Einstein. Sally Field and Suzanne Somers were both born as Mahoney, Ethel Merman and Bob Dylan as Zimmermann and Zimmerman, and Talia Shire and Nicolas Cage as Coppola. Michael Keaton began life as Michael Douglas, while Diane Keaton entered the earthly stage as Diane Hall and played Annie Hall in *Annie Hall*.

Oprah Winfrey was christened Orpah, a biblical name from the Book of Ruth. People unfailingly mispronounced Orpah as Oprah, so she changed it. One of the most famous and successful talk-show hosts ever, she named her production company HARPO, inadvertently referring to the Marx brother who almost never talked—a backwards spelling of her own name.

In the 1940 film *His Girl Friday*, Cary Grant delivered the line "The last person to say that to me was Archie Leach, just before I cut his throat." The inside joke here is that Cary Grant's original name was Archibald Leach.

Would any marquee have been able to accommodate the real names of Dirk Bogarde, Mitzi Gaynor, José Ferrer, Carmen Miranda, and Sophia Loren—Derek Jules Gaspard Ulric Niven van den Bogaerde, Francesca Marlene do Czanyl von Gerber, José Vicente Ferrer da Otero Cintrón, Maria de Carmo Miranda de Cunha, and Sofia Costanza Brigida Villani Scicolone?

Here is a star-studded Walk of Names of twenty-five names-behind-the-names of some of the movie stars who shine brightest in the entertainment heavens:

Fred Astaire	Frederick Austerlitz
Anne Bancroft	Anna Maria Louisa Italiano
Charles Bronson	Karolis Dionyzas Bucinskis
Michael Caine	Maurice Joseph Micklewhite Jr.
Cyd Charisse	Tula Ellice Finklea
Joan Crawford	Lucille Fay LeSueur
Sandra Dee	Alexandra Zuck
Jamie Foxx	Eric Marlon Bishop
Greta Garbo	Greta Lovisa Gustafsson
Judy Garland	Frances Ethel Gumm

James Garner	James Scott Bumgarner
Whoopi Goldberg	Caryn Elaine Johnson
Rita Hayworth	Margarita Carmen Cansino
Rock Hudson	Roy Harold Scherer
Ben Kingsley	Krishna Pandit Bhanji
Karl Malden	Mladen George Sekulovich
Dean Martin	Dino Paul Crocetti
Helen Mirren	Helen Lydia Mironoff
Jack Palance	Volodymyr Palahniuk
Joaquin Phoenix	Joaquin Rafael Bottom
Ginger Rogers	Virginia Kathleen McMath
Mickey Rooney	Joseph Yule Jr.
Robert Taylor	Spangler Arlington Brugh
Raquel Welch	Jo Raquel Tejada
Natalie Wood	Natalia Nikolaevna Zakharenko

Many Jewish entertainers felt they had to Americanize their names. Did you know that Bronco Billy Anderson, the first cowboy movie star, was born Maxwell Henry Aronson, that Marcel Marceau began life as Marcel Mangel, or that Michael Igor Peschkowsky and Elaine Iva Berlin transmogrify into Mike Nichols and Elaine May?

Michael Landon was born Eugene Maurice Orowitz, Winona Rider Winona Laura Horowitz, and three of the actors who played the Three Stooges—Moe, Shemp. and Jerome "Curly" Howard—were originally Horwitzes. All these show people were or are Jewish.

Here are twenty more movie stars' names paired with their Jewish birth names:

Woody Allen	Allen Stewart Konigsberg
Lauren Bacall	Betty Joan Perske
Mel Brooks	Melvin Kaminsky
George Burns	Nathan Birnbaum
Eddie Cantor	Edward Israel Isskowitz
Lee J. Cobb	Leo Jacoby
Tony Curtis	Bernard Schwartz
Rodney Dangerfield	Jacob Cohen
Kirk Douglas	Issur Danielovitch

Laurence Harvey	Laruschka Mischa Skikne
Judy Holiday	Judith Tuvim
Al Jolson	Asa Yoelson
Danny Kaye	David Daniel Kaminsky
Hedy Lamarr	Hedwig Eva Maria Kiesler
Jerry Lewis	Joseph Levitch
Peter Lorre	Laszlo Lowenstein
Natalie Portman	Natalie Hershlag
Edward G. Robinson	Emmanuel Goldenberg
Gene Wilder	Jerome Silberman
Shelly Winters	Shirley Schrift

This transmutation of Jewish names has diminished as an increasing number of Jewish actors have been retaining their birth names.

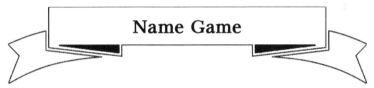

Name Game

If scarlet clothing fasteners yields *Red Buttons* and diet soda seeker *Tab Hunter*, match the following punderful aliases with the celebrity names they suggest:

1. bird metal shoe supports	Armie Hammer
2. car pursuit	Billy Crystal
3. chromosome splicer	Bob Hope
4. conqueror grown up	Brad Pitt
5. crazier chromosome	Brooke Shields
6. crimson bones	Chevy Chase
7. insect monarch fuel	Christian Bale
8. Jesus-loving cotton unit	Gene Hackman
9. male cat on a ship	Gene Wilder
10. male goat quartz	Glenn Close
11. military branch tool	Heath Ledger
12. nail fruit seed	Jay Silverheels
13. nearby valley	Jim Carrey
14. steal the blackbird	John Candy
15. steal from the bottom	Minnie Driver

16. stone river	Minnie Pearl
17. stream protectors	Nat King Cole
18. tear ripped	Red Skelton
19. tiny auto operator	Rip Torn
20. tiny gemstone	Rob Lowe
21. toilet confection	Rock Hudson
22. toilet meadows	Russell Crowe
23. tote the workout space	Tom Cruise
24. tract account book	Victor Mature
25. what fisherpeople live on	W. C. Fields

Answers

1. Jay Silverheels 2. Chevy Chase 3. Gene Hackman 4. Victor Mature 5. Gene Wilder

6. Red Skelton 7. Nat King Cole 8. Christian Bale 9. Tom Cruise 10. Billy Crystal

11. Armie Hammer 12. Brad Pitt 13. Glenn Close 14. Russell Crowe 15. Rob Lowe

16. Rock Hudson 17. Brooke Shields 18. Rip Torn 19 Minnie Driver 20. Minnie Pearl

21. John Candy 22. W. C. Fields 23. Jim Carrey 24. Heath Ledger 25. Bob Hope

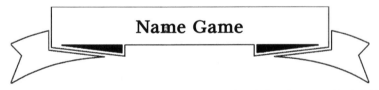

Name Game

Identify each power couple described by the following punderful blend words:

1. Bennifer 2. Billary 3. Brady Bundch 4. Brangelina 5. Kimye 6. Tom Kat

Answers

1. Ben Afflek and Jennifer Lopez 2. Bill and Hillary Clinton 3. Tom Brady and Giselle Bundchen 4. Brad Pitt and Angelina Jolie 5. Kim Kardashian and Kanye West 6. Tom Cruise and Katie Holmes

What's in a President's Name?

U.S. Grant

Being president is like running a cemetery:
You've got a lot of people under you, and nobody's listening.
—BILL CLINTON

We live in a country in which anyone can become president of the United States. Jefferson was president. Nixon was president. Truman was president. Heck, any Tom, Dick, and Harry can be president!

The names of seven of our American presidents changed between birth and prominence:

Ulysses S. Grant came into this world as Hiram Ulysses Grant. When his name was mistakenly entered on the West Point register as *Ulysses S. Grant* (the *S.* was for *Simpson*, his mother's maiden name), he eagerly embraced the error because he detested the initials *H. U. G.* and loved having the initials *U.S.*, which stood for "United States," "Uncle Sam," and, twenty years later, "Unconditional Surrender."

Which president was born a king?

Born Leslie Lynch King Jr., Gerald R. Ford Jr. took the name of his adoptive father after his mother's divorce. Similarly, William Jefferson Clinton was born William Jefferson Blythe III three months after his father died in an automobile accident. When his mother wed Roger Clinton, he took the family name.

Less pyrotechnically, Grover was originally the middle name of Stephen Grover Cleveland, Woodrow the middle name of Thomas Woodrow Wilson, Calvin the middle name of John Calvin Coolidge, and Dwight the middle name of David Dwight Eisenhower.

What is the most popular first name among presidents? The answer is James. Six presidents share that first name—Madison, Monroe, Polk, Buchanan, Garfield, and Carter. Tied for second place are William with four—Harrison, McKinley, Taft, and Clinton—and John with four—Adams, Quincy Adams, Tyler, and Kennedy.

Despite fourteen presidents with the first names James, John, and William, twenty of our chief executives, starting with Thomas Jefferson and ending with Donald Trump, have first names not shared by any other man in the office.

Five pairs of presidents have shared the same last name—John Adams and his son John Quincy, William Henry Harrison and his grandson Benjamin, Theodore Roosevelt and his fifth cousin Franklin, and George H.

W. Bush and his son George W. Only Andrew and Lyndon Johnson were unrelated to each other.

Here are some other letter-perfect tidbits of presidential nomenclature:

Five presidential last names consist of four letters. In chronological order, they are Polk, Taft, Ford, Bush, and Bush. George W. Bush is the only one among them to have served two terms.

In contrast to the monosyllabic monikers above, *Eisenhower* is the only presidential surname that contains four syllables.

Obama is the only presidential surname that begins and ends with a vowel.

S is the most common letter at the beginning of English words and last names, but no president's surname starts with that letter. The letters *J* and *T* start the last names of nine presidents—Thomas Jefferson, Andrew Jackson, Andrew Johnson, and Lyndon Johnson and John Tyler, Zachary Taylor, William Howard Taft, Harry Truman, and Donald Trump.

Only one president's name contains a letter that is found in no other president's name. That letter is the *q* in John Quincy Adams.

Ulysses Simpson Grant and Rutherford Birchard Hayes are the only presidential names that contain *a, e, i, o,* and *u,* with a *y* to boot.

Four presidents have had alliterative names—Woodrow Wilson, Calvin Coolidge, Herbert Hoover, and Ronald Reagan. They all served in the twentieth century.

Pierce, Grant, Hoover (in England), Ford, Carter, Bush, and Trump are all common English words when uncapitalized.

An anagram is the rearrangement of all the letters in a word or phrase to create another word of phrase. Here, in chronological order, are the best efforts to anagram the names of our twentieth- and twenty-first-century presidents. Some work better grammatically than others; some are more appropriate to the president, some less telling.

Theodore Roosevelt	LOVED HORSE, TREE, TOO.
William Howard Taft	A WORD WITH ALL: I'M FAT.
Woodrow Wilson	O LORD, SO NOW WWI.
Warren Gamaliel Harding	WINNER? HIM A REAL LAGGARD.
Calvin Coolidge	LOVE? A COLD ICING.
Herbert Clark Hoover	O, HARK, CLEVER BROTHER.
Franklin Delano Roosevelt	ELEANOR, KIN, LAST FOND LOVER
Harry S. Truman	RASH ARMY RUNT

Dwight David Eisenhower	HE DID VIEW THE WAR DOINGS.
John Fitzgerald Kennedy	ZING! JOY DARKEN, THEN FLED.
Lyndon Baines Johnson	NO NINNY, HE'S ON JOB, LADS.
Richard Milhous Nixon	HUSH—NIX CRIMINAL ODOR!
Gerald Rudolph Ford	A RUDER LORD; GOLF PH.D
James Earl Carter	A RARE, CALM JESTER
Ronald W. Reagan	A WAN OLD RANGER
George Bush	HE BUGS GORE.
William Jefferson Clinton	JILTS NICE WOMEN; IN FOR FALL
George W. Bush	HE GREW BOGUS / WE GUSH OR BEG.
Barack Hussein Obama	ABRAHAM IS BACK. ONE U.S.!
Donald Trump	DUMP TAN LORD.

Presidents have more than their share of intriguing middle names.

Two of them—Ronald *Wilson* Reagan and William *Jefferson* Clinton—match the last names of two of their predecessors.

And then there's Harry S. Truman—or is it Harry S Truman, without the period?

Truman initiated this punctuation controversy in 1962, when he told reporters that the *S* wasn't an initial for a particular name. Rather, the *S* was a compromise between the names of his grandfathers, Anderson Shipp Truman and Solomon Young, making the letter a kind of embracive middle name.

But Truman himself usually placed a period after the *S*, and the most authoritative style manuals recommend its use in the interest of consistency, even if the initial does not appear to stand for any particular name.

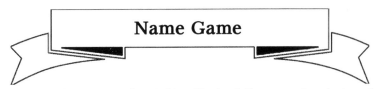

Name Game

Using each middle name listed, identify the full name of each American president:

1. Abram
2. Alan
3. Baines
4. Birchard
5. Clark

9. Gamaliel
10. Henry
11. Herbert Walker
12. Howard
13. Knox

6. Delano
7. Earl
8. Fitzgerald

14. Milhous
15. Quincy
16. Walker

Answers

1. James Abram Garfield 2. Chester Alan Arthur 3. Lyndon Baines Johnson 4. Rutherford Birchard Hayes 5. Herbert Clark Hoover 6. Franklin Delano Roosevelt 7. James Earl Carter 8. John Fitzgerald Kennedy

9. Warren Gamaliel Harding 10. William Henry Harrison 11. George Herbert Walker Bush (our only president to be identified with two middle names) 12. William Howard Taft 13. James Knox Polk 14. Richard Milhous Nixon 15. John Quincy Adams 16. George Walker Bush

In New England in the 1830s, there was a craze for initialisms, in the manner of *FYI, PDQ, aka,* and *TGIF,* so popular today. The fad went so far as to generate letter combinations of intentionally comic misspellings: *KG* for "know go," *KY* for "know yuse," *NSMJ* for "'nough said 'mong jentlemen," and *OR* for "oll rong."*OK* for "oll korrect" naturally followed.

Of all those loopy initialisms and facetious misspellings *OK* alone survived. That's because of a presidential nickname that consolidated the letters in the national memory. Martin Van Buren, elected our eighth president in 1836, was born in Kinderhook, New York, and early in his political career was dubbed "Old Kinderhook." Echoing the "Oll Korrect" initialism, *OK* became the rallying cry of the Old Kinderhook Club, a Democratic organization supporting Van Buren during the 1840 campaign. Thus, the accident of Van Buren's birthplace saved *OK* from the dustbin of history.

The coinage did Van Buren no good, and he was defeated in his bid for reelection. But the word honoring his name today remains what H. L. Mencken identified as "the most shining and successful Americanism ever invented."

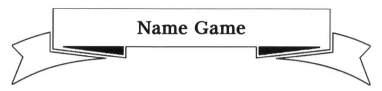

Name Game

Match the presidential nicknames in the right-hand column with the appropriate presidents in the left-hand column:

1.	James Buchanan	The Bachelor President
2.	Bill Clinton	Big Bill
3.	Calvin Coolidge	Bubba
4.	Dwight Eisenhower	The Father of His Country
5.	Ulysses S. Grant	The Gipper
6.	William Henry Harrison	The Great Emancipator
7.	Andrew Jackson	The Haberdasher
8.	Thomas Jefferson	His Accidency
9.	John F. Kennedy	Ike
10.	Abraham Lincoln	The King of Camelot
11.	Richard Nixon	The New Dealer
12.	Ronald Reagan	Old Hickory
13.	Franklin Roosevelt	Old Rough and Ready
14.	Theodore Roosevelt	The Rough Rider
15.	William Howard Taft	The Sage of Monticello
16.	Zachary Taylor	The Schoolmaster
17.	Harry Truman	Silent Cal
18.	John Tyler	Tippecanoe
19.	George Washington	Tricky Dicky
20.	Woodrow Wilson	Unconditional Surrender

Answers

1. The Bachelor President 2. Bubba 3. Silent Cal 4. Ike 5. Unconditional Surrender

6. Tippecanoe 7. Old Hickory 8. The Sage of Monticello 9. The King of Camelot 10. The Great Emancipator

11. Tricky Dicky 12. The Gipper 13. The New Dealer 14. The Rough Rider 15. Big Bill

16. Old Rough and Ready 17. The Haberdasher 18. His Accidency 19. The Father of His Country 20. The Schoolmaster

Immortal Mortals

Etienne de Silhouette

Tigers die and leave their skins.
People die and leave their names.
—JAPANESE PROVERB

Live so that you beautify your name,
even if it wasn't beautiful to begin with,
making it stand in people's thoughts
for something so lovely and pleasant
that they never think of it by itself.
—L. M. MONTGOMERY

Here lies one whose name was writ on water.
—JOHN KEATS

In previous chapters of this book you have seen how people get their names from words already in our language. Now let's consider how the kinship works in both directions, how common words are forged from proper names. These words lose their reference to specific persons and become generic terms in our dictionaries, and when they do, they usually shed their capital letters. Such additions to our vocabulary help our language to remain alive and growing, muscular and energetic.

In ancient times, the gods snatched up the souls of those mortals who had found favor in their eyes and made them into stars so that they could forever shine in the heavens for humankind to see. Some men and women have likewise been endowed with a measure of immortality by having their names transmuted into everyday words because of a discovery, object, deed, or attribute of character associated with them.

The Greeks had a word for people who live on in our everyday conversations—*eponymos*, from which we derive the word *eponym*, meaning "after or upon a name." Thousands of eponyms teem our tongues and dot our dictionaries. Stories of the origins of words made from real or imaginary people are among the richest and most entertaining in our language:

In pre-revolutionary France there lived one Etienne de Silhouette, a controller-general for Louis XV. Because of his fanatical zeal for raising taxes and slashing expenses and pensions, he enraged royalty and citizens alike, who ran him out of office within eight months.

At about the same time that the penny-pinching Silhouette was sacked for his infuriating parsimony, the method of making cutouts of profile portraits by throwing the shadow of the subject on the screen captured the fancy of the Paris public. Because the process was cheap and one that cut back to absolute essentials (a scissors and maybe a knife), the man and the method, in the spirit of ridicule, became associated. Ever since, we have called shadow profiles *silhouettes*, with a lowercase *s*.

***

The life and writings of the Donatien Alphonse François, Marquis de Sade extolled the pleasures of inflicting sexual pain. The marquis lives on through the word sadism. From Austrian novelist Leopold Sacher-Masoch, whose fictional characters enjoyed receiving pain, we derive the word *masochism*.

As the sardonic joke goes, the masochist says, "Beat me! Beat me!" And the sadist replies, "No."

***

> Four noble earls, whom, if I quote,
> Some folks might call me sinner.
> One's name's a hat, two names are coats.
> The fourth one's half a dinner.

Edward Stanley, 12th Earl of Derby, founded a horse race at Epson Downs. It and many subsequent races bear his name as does the round hat often sported at such events.

Philip Dormer Stanhope, 4th Earl of Chesterfield, and James Thomas Brudenell, 7th Earl of Cardigan, bequeathed us the Chesterfield and cardigan jackets.

In order to spend more uninterrupted time at the gambling tables, John Montagu, 4th Earl of Sandwich, ordered his servants to bring him an impromptu meal of slices of beef slapped between two slices of bread. Thus, one of our favorite repasts is named after a compulsive gambler.

***

Late in the nineteenth century, a daydreaming British preppie named Edmund Clerihew Bentley gave the world a new form of nonsense verse. Author of the novel *Trent's Last Case*, Bentley is also remembered as the inventor of the clerihew. Bentley's son, Nicholas, wrote, "I think it gave him more pleasure than anything else he achieved in life that he lived to see the word *clerihew* enshrined in the *Oxford Dictionary* as part of our language."

When Bentley was twelve, he was enrolled at St. Paul's School, the famous London boys' school. It was there in 1891, when he was sixteen, that, to pass the time in a study hall, he concocted his first clerihew:

> Sir Humphrey Davy
> Abominated gravy.
> He lived in the odium
> Of having invented sodium.

The clerihew is a whimsical, pseudo-biographical quatrain rhymed (often outrageously) as two couplets with short, pithy lines of uneven length and meter. The name of the individual who is the subject of the quatrain usually supplies the first line, as in this creation of mine:

> Edmund Clerihew Bentley
> Wrote light verses expediently,
> For which he became rather famous.
> That fellow was no ignoramus.

And here's one that I've written immodestly about myself:

> Richard Henry Lederer
> Will undangle your participle, etceterer.
> In a manner most definitive,
> He'll also unsplit your infinitive.

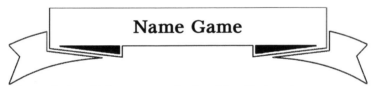

Name Game

Here is a quiz in which you are asked to identify twenty common words and the names of the immortal mortals from whom they descend. May this challenge not turn you into a masochistic dunce but rather galvanize you to platonic heights of onomastic achievement:

1. In 1812, Elbridge _____, governor of Massachusetts, became the inspiration for a political term in our English language. In an effort to sustain his party's power, Gerry divided his state into electoral districts with more regard to politics than to geographical reality.

To a drawing of one of the governor's manipulated districts Gilbert Stuart—the same fellow who had painted the famous portrait of George Washington—added a head, eyes, wings, and claws. According to one version of the story, Stuart exclaimed about his creation, "That looks like a salamander!"

"No," countered the editor of the newspaper in which the cartoon was to appear, "Better call it a ____!"

The verb ____ is still used today to describe the shaping of electoral entities for political gain.

2. Samuel Augustus ____, a San Antonio rancher, acquired vast tracts of land and dabbled in cattle raising. When he neglected to brand the calves born into his herd, his neighbors began calling the unmarked off-spring by his name. Through a process that linguists call generalization, this word has come to designate any nonconformist.

3. ____, the name of a courageous Apache warrior chief, became a battle cry for World War II paratroopers.

4. Amelia Jenks ____ was an American feminist who helped to publi-cize the fashionable puffy ladies drawers that seemed to bloom like linen flowers.

5. Charles Cunningham ____, an Irish land agent, so enraged his tenants with his rent-collection policies that they threatened his life and property and burnt his figure in effigy. Hence, from Ireland comes the verb that means "to coerce an opponent through ostracism."

6. Franz Anton ____, a Viennese physician, attempted to treat his patients by fixing them with a piercing gaze, questioning them about their ailments, and stroking them with a wand. Today, a form of his name means "to hypnotize, to fascinate."

7. The Rev. William Archibald ____, head of New College, Oxford, set out to become a birdwatcher but instead became a word-botcher. He became renowned for his hilarious reversals of sounds and syllables, such as "You are occupewing my pie. May I sew you to another sheet?" and "Three cheers for our queer old dean."

8. Nicholas ____, a veteran soldier in the French First Republic and Empire, was ridiculed by his comrades for his excessive devotion to the defeated Napoleon. First used as a synonym for knee-jerk patriotism, his name was picked up during the 1970s by the feminist movement to sig-nify attitudes of male supremacy.

9. A century before Elvis Presley, the handsome face of Civil War gen-eral Ambrose E. ____ was adorned by luxuriant side-whiskers sweeping down from his ears to his clean-shaven chin.

10. Dame Nellie ____, a famous Australian coloratura soprano, be-came so much the toast of the town that a toast was named after her, as well as a peachy dessert.

11. The Marquise de ____, mistress of King Louis XV, wore her hair swept straight up from the forehead in a style that became the rage of

the women of Paris.

12. The European hotels of Swiss magnate Cesar _____ were so swanky that his surname is now eponymously synonymous with high-class lodgings.

13. A snugly fitting body garment worn by dancers and acrobats descends from the name of Jules _____, a widely acclaimed French trapeze artist who was the first to perfect the aerial somersault.

14. A colorful plant characterized by scarlet leaves is especially popular at Christmastime. This Christmas flower takes its name from Joel R. _____, America's first ambassador to Mexico, who introduced the plant to the United States from its native land.

15. In the New Testament, Mary _____ devotedly followed Jesus and ministered to his needs. Portraits of her by Giotto, Titian, Veronese, and many other artists unfailingly depict her as weeping. From her name we derive an adjective that means "tearfully sentimental."

16. British engineer John L. _____ invented a durable material for repairing roads. We use his name for both the material and the act of applying it.

17. The sixteenth-century followers of the philosopher John _____ Scotus were sneered at because they clung to their old beliefs instead of accepting the "new learning." Even though this philosopher was quite intelligent, we use a variation of his middle name to label people we think are stupid.

18. Dr. Thomas _____ of London was a self-appointed literary censor who published a diluted version of Shakespeare for family consumption. A form of his name has become synonymous with watering down art so as not to offend delicate sensibilities.

19. Luigi _____ was an Italian physiologist who stimulated sudden movement in frogs' legs by touching them with static electricity. Today a form of his name means to stimulate into action, as if with an electrical charge.

20. Sylvester _____, an American dietary reformer, donated to our language the name of a cracker made of ground whole wheat flour.

Answers

1. gerrymander-Gerry 2. maverick-Maverick 3. Geronimo!-Geronimo 4. bloomers-Bloomer 5. boycott-Boycott

6. mesmerize-Mesmer 7. spoonerism-Spooner 8. chauvinism-Chauvin 9. sideburns-Burnside 10. Melba toast, Peach Melba (a rare double play!)-Melba

11. pompadour-Pompadour 12. ritzy, the ritz-Ritz 13. leotard-Leotard 14. poinsettia-Poinsett (Please don't spell the name of the flower as point-settia, pointsetta, or poinsetta.) 15. maudlin-Mary Magdalen

16. macadam, macadamize-McAdam 17. dunce-Duns 18. bowdlerize-Bowdler 19. galvanize-Galvani 20. graham cracker-Graham

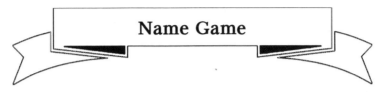

Name Game

What do the following names have in common?: Andre-Marie Ampere, Henry Brougham, Samuel Colt, Thomas Derrick, George Washington Gale Ferris Jr., T. D. Gimlette, Joseph-Ignace Guillotin, R. J. L. Guppy, Charles Lynch, Jean Nicot, Louis Pasteur, Vidkun Quisling, Allessandro Volta, Jean Martinet, and James Watt.

Answer

They are all eponyms.

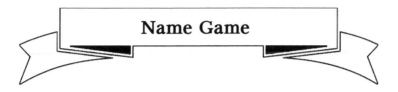

Name Game

The surest way to grab yourself a place in the English language is to invent a gadget so original and useful that people will have to call it by your name, often lowercased. Here are the names of fifteen clever inventors who have done just that. Briefly identify what each of the men below invented:

1. Jim Bowie
2. Robert Wilhelm Bunsen
3. Louis Daguerre
4. Henry Derringer
5. Rudolph Diesel
6. Richard Gatling
7. Johannes Wilhelm Geiger
8. Joseph Hansom
9. Charles McIntosh
10. John Mason
11. George Pullman
12. Henry Shrapnel
13. John Philip Sousa
14. Oliver Winchester
15. Ferdinand, Count von Zeppelin

Answers

1. Bowie knife 2. Bunsen burner 3. daguerreotype (photographic process) 4. derringer pistol 5. diesel engine 6. Gatling gun 7. Geiger counter 8. Hansom carriage 9. MackIntosh raincoat 10. Mason jar 11. Pullman railroad car 12. shrapnel (shell fragments) 13. sousaphone 14. Winchester rifle 15. Zeppelin airship

Names Throw
the Book at Us

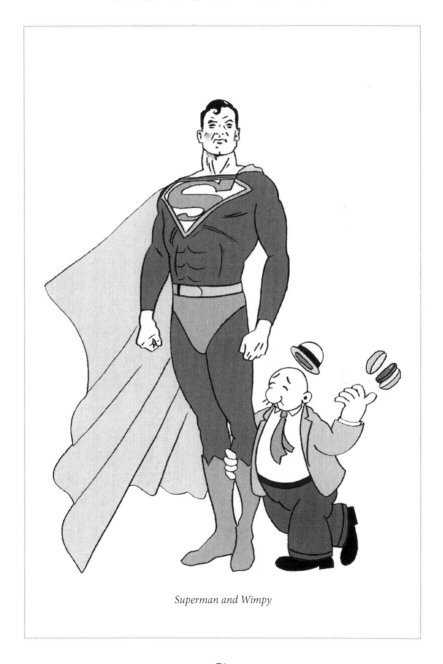

Superman and Wimpy

It is not true that we have only one life to live.
If we can read, we have as many more lives
and kinds of lives as we wish.
—S. I. HAYAKAWA

Another species of eponym is the names of literary characters who step off the pages of books and newspapers to become the generic epithets for well-known types of people. These people are literally and literarily born at the tip of a pen. Fictional though they may be, literary creations can assume a vitality and longevity that pulse as powerfully as human beings.

From the Bible, an old man is a Methuselah, a strong man a Samson, a long-suffering person a Job, a wise man a Solomon, a person who brings bad luck a Jonah, a skeptic a Doubting Thomas, a lascivious woman a Jezebel, and a betrayer of friends a Judas. Indeed, the San Diego Chargers football team, who heartlessly abandoned San Diego, where your author lives, we now call the Los Angeles Judases.

From other literary contexts, a man in pursuit of the ladies is a Romeo, a Don Juan, or a Lothario. A mean-spirited miser is labeled a Scrooge, a usurer a Shylock, a clever deducer a Sherlock Holmes, a hard taskmaster a Simon Legree, and a smug, middle-class conformist a Babbitt.

We call an indispensable helper a man or girl Friday, a person who never wants to grow up a Peter Pan, a foolish optimist a Pollyanna, one who is out of step with his times a Rip Van Winkle, one who exerts sinister control over another a Svengali, two nearly identical males a Tweedledum and Tweedledee, a man with a split personality a Jekyll and Hyde, and an annoyingly obedient person a Goody Two-shoes.

***

When people misuse words in a pretentious but humorous manner, we call the result a *malapropism*. The word echoes the name of Mrs. Malaprop (from the French *mal a propos*, "not appropriate"), a character who first strode the stage in 1775 in Richard Brinsley Sheridan's comedy *The Rivals*. Mrs. Malaprop was a garrulous "old weather-beaten she dragon" who took special pride in her use of the King's English but who, all the same, unfailingly mangled big words: "Sure, if I reprehend anything in this world it is the use of my oracular tongue, and a nice derangement of epitaphs!" She meant, of course, that if she comprehended anything, it was a nice arrangement of epithets.

From *The Rivals*, here are more of Mrs. M's most malapropiate malapropisms:

- Then, sir, she should have a supercilious knowledge in account, and as she grew up, I should have her instructed in geometry, that she might know something of the contagious countries.
- She's as headstrong as an allegory on the banks of the Nile.
- Illiterate him, I say, quite from your memory.
- He's the very pineapple of politeness.

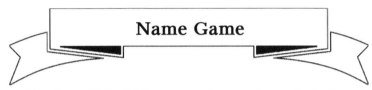

Name Game

The giddy ghost of Mrs. Malaprop continues to haunt the hollowed halls of language. Here are some authentic, certified, unretouched modern-day malapropisms. As Dave Barry, my fellow Haverford College alumnus, would say, I'm not making these up.

Your mission, should you choose to accept it, is to identify the right word that the speaker or writer has mangled:

1. I am privileged to speak at this millstone in the history of the college.
2. In Venice, the people travel around the canals in gorgonzolas.
3. I don't want to cast asparagus at my opponent.
4. Who do you think you are, some kind of hexagon of virtue?
5. We have to deal seriously with this offense as a detergent to others.
6. He died interstate.
7. Too many Americans lead a sedimentary life.
8. The deceased was a vicarious reader.
9. They've decided to raise my benefits, and they're making them radioactive.
10. The only sure-fire way to avoid teenage pregnancy is through obstinance.
11. If you wish to submit a recipe for publication in the cookbook, please include a short antidote concerning it.
12. The mountain is named for the Reverend Starr King, who was an invertebrate climber.
13. The fun and excitement of childhood are nothing compared to the fun and excitement of adultery.

14. Ortiz is the most recent recipient of the pretentious Con Edison Athlete of the Week Award.
15. Senators are chosen as committee chairmen on the basis of senility.
16. I refuse to answer that question. It's too suppository.
17. I took up aerobics to help maintain my well-propositioned figure.
18. Medieval cathedrals were supported by flying buttocks.
19. The marriage was consummated on the altar.
20. The food in our cafeteria is so bad it's not fit for human constipation.

Answers
1. milestone 2. gondolas 3. aspersions 4. paragon 5. deterrent
6. intestate 7. sedentary 8. voracious 9. retroactive 10. abstinence
11. anecdote 12. inveterate 13. adulthood 14. prestigious 15. seniority
16. suppositious 17. proportioned 18. buttresses 19. consecrated 20. consumption

English is a cheerfully hospitable language that welcomes into its realm words near and far, ancient and modern, and of high and low station. It's no surprise, then, that folkloric characters from cartoons, comic strips, and comic books have leapt from the newspapers and screen into our everyday speech and writing.

In 1928, Walt Disney gave the world a Mickey—an all-American rodent who performed heroic deeds and squeaked his undying love for Minnie. Soon after World War II, international markets were flooded with wristwatches bearing Mickey's likeness. Because these watches were generally cheap affairs subject to mechanical breakdowns, people started calling anything shoddy or trivial Mickey Mouse.

The name of H. T. Webster's wimpy comic-strip character, Caspar Milquetoast, has become a synonym for a wimpy, unassertive man. In a similar vein, some scholars assert that the term *sad sack* to designate a pathetically inept man, especially a soldier, owes its origin to the cartoon character created by George Baker in 1942.

Speaking of *wimpy*, some linguists trace *wimpy* to Elzie Segar's cartoon strip *Thimble Theatre,* which, when animated became *Popeye.* Wimpy was a mild-mannered, soft-spoken, lazy, parsimonious, and utterly gluttonous hamburger-wolfing straight man to Popeye.

The opposite of a wimpy person would be a Superman, the comic book creation of Jerry Siegel and Joe Schuster. Faster than a speeding bullet! More powerful than a locomotive! Able to leap tall buildings in a single bound! Superman has become a superman, a person who exhibits extraordinary powers.

Schuster and Siegel purloined the name Superman from the German philosopher Friedrich Nietzsche's Ubermensch, meaning "overman" in *Thus Spake Zarathustra* and George Bernard Shaw's translation of the term in his play *Man and Superman*. Only diehard trivia buffs know that Superman's alter ego, the mild-mannered Clark Kent, derived his name from two 1930s movie stars—the iconic Clark Gable and the never-heard-of-him Kent Taylor.

On the fritz, meaning "not operating properly," may have started with one of the earliest comic strips, *The Katzenjammer Kids*. Typically, the two hyperactive German boys, Hans and Fritz, caused all sorts of troubles for the Captain and other grownups in the story.

Two men of strikingly disparate height are dubbed Mutt and Jeff. The original mustachioed twosome, one tall, one short, inhabited a comic strip by Bud Fisher—the third created in the United States.

For more than eight decades, Blondie's husband has been creating culinary masterpieces in the kitchen, yet he doesn't appear to have gained an ounce (for which I envy him). Dagwood carries the cornucopia of ingredients from the refrigerator to the kitchen table on his arms and head, and the massive repasts he concocts are now known as *Dagwood sandwiches*.

There's a God
in Your Sentence

Zeus and Echo

These old, old stories,
which have been living now for three thousand years,
still penetrate our daily lives.
By understanding these myths, we understand ourselves better.

—ISAAC ASIMOV

O f all the literary sources that feed into our English language, mythology is one of the richest. The ancient gods, goddesses, heroes, and heroines are not dead. We who are alive today constantly speak and hear and write and read their names, even if we don't always know it.

Echo, for example, is an echo of a story that is three millennia old. Echo was a beautiful nymph who once upon a time aided Zeus in a love affair by keeping Hera, his wife, occupied in conversation. As a punishment for such verbal meddling, Hera confiscated Echo's power to initiate conversation and allowed her to repeat only the last words of anything she heard.

Such was a sorry enough fate, but later Echo fell madly in love with an exceedingly handsome Greek boy, Narcissus, who, because of Echo's peculiar handicap, would have nothing to do with her. So deeply did the nymph grieve for her unrequited love that she wasted away until nothing was left but her voice, always repeating the last words she heard.

The fate that befell Narcissus explains why his name has been transformed into words like *narcissism* and *narcissistic*, pertaining to extreme self-love. One day Narcissus looked into a still forest lake and beheld his own face in the water, although he did not know it was his. He at once fell in love with the beautiful image on the surface, and he, like Echo, pined away for a love that could never be consummated.

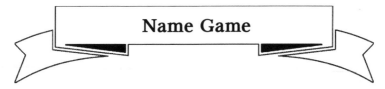

Name Game

Using the following descriptions, identify the gods and goddesses, heroes and heroines, and fabulous creatures that inhabit the world of classical mythology and the words that echo them:

1. One of the vilest of mythology's villains was a king who served the body of his young son to the gods at a feast. They soon discovered the king's wicked ruse, restored the dead boy to life, and devised a punishment to fit the crime. They banished the king to Hades, where he is condemned to stand in a sparkling pool of water with boughs of luscious fruit overhead; when he stoops to drink, the water drains away through the bottom of the pool, and when he wishes to eat, the branches of fruit sway just out of his grasp. Ever since, when something presents itself temptingly to our view, we invoke this king's name.

2. An adjective that means "merry, inspiring mirth" comes from the name the ancient Romans gave to the king of their gods because it was a happy omen to be born under his influence.

3. The frenetic Greek nature god was said to cause sudden fear by darting out from behind bushes and terrifying passers-by. That fear now bears his name.

4. The goddess of love and beauty bequeaths us many words from both her Greek and Roman names.

5. A Greek herald in Homer's *Iliad* was a human public address system, for his voice could be heard all over camp. Today, the adjective form of his name means "loud-voiced, bellowing."

6. The most famous of all of Homer's creations spent ten years after the fall of Troy wandering through the ancient world encountering sorceresses and Cyclopes. The wily hero's name lives on in the word we use to describe a long journey or voyage marked by bizarre turns of events.

7. The aforementioned hero was tempted by mermaids who perched on rocks in the sea and lured ancient mariners to their deaths. Their piercing call has given us our word for the rising and falling whistle emitted by ambulances, fire engines, and police cars.

8. Another great Greek hero needed all his power to complete twelve exceedingly laborious labors. We use a form of his name to describe a

mighty effort or an extraordinarily difficult task.

9. A tribe of female warriors cut off their right breasts in order to handle their bows more efficiently. The name of their tribe originally meant "breastless"; it now means a powerful woman.

10. Because of its fluidity and mobility, quicksilver is identified by a more common label that is the Roman name for Hermes, the winged messenger of the gods. That name has also bequeathed us an adjective meaning "swift, eloquent, volatile."

Answers

1. tantalize-Tantalus 2. jovial-Jove 3. panic-Pan 4. aphrodisiac, hermaphrodite-Aphrodite; venereal, venerate-Venus 5. stentorian-Stentor

6. odyssey-Odysseus 7. siren-the Sirens 8. herculean-Hercules 9. amazon-Amazons 10. mercury, mercurial-Mercury

When the Name
is the Game

Usain Bolt

My name means the shape I am.
—HUMPTY DUMPTY

Names are powerful and are prophecies of the future.
The name you are called is a sign of what you are
and what you would become.
—JUDE IDADA

Names aren't loners, they're connected, even in real life.
You name your kids for someone dead or what you hope they will become
or what you wish you were and your parents did the same to you
and that big, glittering net of names tells the story of the whole world.
Names are load-bearing struts. Names are destiny.
—CATHERYNNE M. VALE

Talk about coincidences. The fastest man in the world ever is the electrifying Usain Bolt, record-setting champion of the 100- and 200-meter dashes who was fast as a greased lightning bolt and who effortlessly bolted ahead of his competitors. Louis Jean and Auguste Marie Lumiere created the first movies that told stories. In French, *Lumiere* means "light." And Margaret Court holds a record twenty-four Grand Slam singles championships in professional tennis. In fact, in Rod Laver stadium in Melbourne, Australia, there is actually a Margaret Court court!

Names such as *Bolt, Lumiere,* and *Court* that are especially suited to the profession or a characteristic of their owners are called aptronyms, a term coined by newspaper columnist Franklin P. Adams. Believe it or not, Dan Druff is or was a barber, C. Sharpe Minor the preeminent organ accompanist to silent films, Fanny Hard a corset saleswoman, Charles Will Fillerup an owner of a gas station, Muffin Fry a baker, Scott Free a defense attorney, Robert Supena a lawyer, Lee Popwell a chiropractor, Tony Buzz us a beekeeper, and Walter Wall a carpet salesman.

Sarah Blizzard, Amy Freeze, Dallas Raines, and Larry Sprinkle are real-life meteorologists. Doctors D. Kaye, Fang, Pullem, Filler, Fillmore, Gumm, Spitz, Tartar, Toothaker, Toothman, Hertz, and Payne are real-life dentists.

The funeral parlor business attracts a number of people with apt nomenclature, including Wake Doom, Groaner Digger, Frank Deadman, Virgil Berriman, Fillmore Graves, Jay Posthumas, C. D'eath, and W. A. Coldflesh.

Add to that line-up Doctor Doctor Willard Bliss. No, that's not a misprint. Doctor was Bliss's given first name, and he grew up to become a doctor and expert in ballistic trauma. In fact, he headed a team that, in 1881, unsuccessfully treated James Garfield after the president's mortal wounding by an assassin's bullet.

Some observers believe that names like Usain Bolt, Sarah Blizzard, Virgil Buryman, and Doctor Bliss can influence the job that its grown-up owner chooses. The theory even has a name: nominative determinism.

Freakonomics authors Steven Leavitt and Stephen Dubner put it this way: "Does the name you give your child affect his life? Or is *your* life reflected in his name? Singing icon Madonna answers, "How could I have been anything else but what I am, having been named Madonna. I would either have ended up a nun or this." Sociologist Adam Alter explains, "It's possible that you are drawn to what your name keeps reminding you about."

In either case, what kind of signal does a child's name send to the world—and most important, does it really matter?

Here's a list of famous aptronymic personages:

- football star Jim Kiick;

- baseball stars Early Wynn, Herb Score, Johnny Bench, Jeff Bagwell, and Cecil and Prince Fielder;

- golf greats Gary Player and Tiger Woods;

- basketball great Tim Duncan;

- long-distance swimmer Diana Nyad (a naiad is a water nymph, and NAIAD is an anagram of DIANA);

- U.S. soccer coach Bruce Arena;

- astronaut Sally Ride;

- presidential spokesperson for Ronald Reagan Larry Speakes;

- romantic poet William Wordsworth;

- World Series of Poker champions Jamie Gold and Chris Moneymaker;

- TV host of the heart-strings-tugging series "On the Road" Steve Hartman;

- financial guru Bernie Madoff, who infamously made off with billions of dollars of other people's money;

- Rich Fairbank, founder and CEO of Capital One Financial Corporation;

- James Cash Penney, founder of the J.C. Penney stores;

- Marilyn vos Savant, a popular columnist who has been cited for owning the world's highest recorded IQ;
- Learned Hand, American judge;
- manufacturer of flush toilets Thomas Crapper;
- Gershon Legman, editor of fat volumes of bawdy limericks;
- Anthony Weiner, politician involved in multiple sex scandals;
- and spouse snipper Lorena Bobbitt (Get it? "Bob it.").

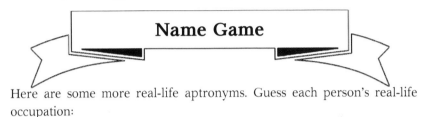

Name Game

Here are some more real-life aptronyms. Guess each person's real-life occupation:

1. Steve Adore
2. James Bugg
3. Henry Ford Carr
4. Bill Dollar
5. Storm Field
6. William Headline
7. Turner Heaton
8. Les Plack
9. Alto Reed
10. Summer Starfield
11. John Wisdom
12. Sue Yoo

Answers

1. dock worker 2. exterminator 3. automobile salesman 4. accountant 5. meteorologist 6. journalist

7. plumber 8. dentist 9. saxophonist 10. astronomer 11. philosopher 12. lawyer

Close kin to aptronyms are charactonyms, names of literary characters that are especially suited to their personality. The enormous and enduring popularity of Charles Dickens's works springs in part from the writer's skill at creating memorable charactonyms—Scrooge, the tight-fisted miser; Mr. Gradgrind, the tyrannical schoolmaster; Jaggers, the rough-edged lawyer; the toady Uriah Heep, the sanctimonious Seth Pecksniff, and Miss Havisham ("have a sham"), the jilted spinster who lives lost in an illusion. John Bunyan's Mr. Worldly Wiseman, Henry Fielding's Squire Allworthy, Susanna Centlivre's Simon Pure, and Walter Scott's Dr. Dryasdust are other prominent charactonyms.

Modern examples include Willie Loman ("low man") in Arthur Miller's *Death of a Salesman,* Jim Trueblood in Ralph Ellison's *Invisible Man,* and comic-strip matriarch Mary Worth. In the 1970s, a doctor show named *Marcus Welby* ruled the television ratings. The title and name of the lead character were purposely designed to make us think of "make us well be."

Same Names of Fame

Giuseppe Verdi

> THIRD PLEBEIAN: Your name, sir, truly.
> CINNA: Truly, my name is Cinna.
> FIRST PLEBEIAN: Tear him to pieces! He's a conspirator!
> *CINNA: I am Cinna the poet, I am Cinna the poet.*
> *I am not Cinna the conspirator.*
> *FOURTH PLEBEIAN: It is no matter, his name's Cinna.*
> *Pluck but his name out of his heart, and turn him going.*
> *THIRD PLEBEIAN: Tear him, tear him!*
> —WILLIAM SHAKESPEARE, *Julius Caesar*

Have you ever noticed that certain historical personages and other famous men and women occasionally share identical, or very similar, first and last names? Singer-songwriter Paul Simon and Illinois senator Paul Simon. *Garfield* creator Jim Davis and North Carolina senator Jim Davis. Broadcasting mogul Larry King and Larry King, tennis promoter and former husband of Billie Jean King. Oscar winner Anne Hathaway and Renaissance woman Anne Hathaway, the wife of William Shakespeare. Actor Jane Seymour and Jane Seymour, a wife of Henry VIII.

Once you home in on this concept, same-name twins—and a few triplets—pop up everywhere: Television anchor Robin Roberts and pitching great Robin Roberts. Explorer Richard Burton and actor Richard Burton. New York mayor Robert Wagner and actor Robert Wagner. Golfer John Daly and *What's My Line* host John Daly. Outlaw Jesse James, professional football player Jesse James, and reality-show star Jesse James.

Also stepping forward: Comedian Dave Thomas and the founder of Wendy's, Dave Thomas. Actor Matthew Perry and explorer Matthew Perry. Inventor James Watt and Secretary of the Interior James Watt. Alabama Governor George Wallace and stand-up comedian George Wallace.

Next appear names that vary only by spelling, nickname, or an added initial: Novelist Thomas Wolfe and novelist Tom Wolfe. Actor James Dean and country singer and sausage maker Jimmy Dean. Tycoon J. P. Morgan and singer Jaye P. Morgan. Secretary of State James Baker and evangelist Jim Bakker. Playwright and poet Ben Jonson and sprinter Ben Johnson. Playwright George Bernard Shaw and newscaster Bernard Shaw. Congressman and civil rights activist John Lewis and union leader John L. Lewis. Quarterback Randall Cunningham and California congressman Randall "Duke" Cunningham. Pop superstar Ricky Martin and *Laugh-In* comedian Dick Martin. Comedian Jerry Lewis and singer Jerry Lee Lewis.

On a personal note, when I, Richard H. Lederer, began publishing my words about words, I started receiving mail intended for one Richard M. Lederer Jr., a well-known historical linguist.

If you really strain your brain, you'll uncover a clutch of same-name triplets, especially the Jones boys: Financial adviser Edward Jones, British racecar driver Ed Jones, and football star Ed "Too Tall" Jones. Actor James Earl Jones, novelist James Jones, and cult leader Jim Jones. Golfer Bobby Jones, golf course architect Robert Trent Jones, and evangelist Bob Jones. Henry Fielding hero Tom Jones, singer Tom Jones, and actor Tommy Lee Jones. Add to those triads soul singer James Brown, sports commentator James Brown, and football great/actor Jim Brown. Actor Robert Shaw, chorale leader Robert Shaw, and abolitionist/Civil War colonel Robert Gould Shaw.

Now the language limelight shines upon a category that will appeal especially to wordplay lovers. These groupings embrace fictional characters, pseudonyms, homophonic names, and foreign-language equivalents.

Here we are entertained by heroic Dickensian orphan David Copperfield and magician David Copperfield. Dickensian urchin Tiny Tim and weird singer Tiny Tim. Art Carney character Ed Norton and actor Ed Norton. *Gunsmoke* marshal Matt Dillon and actor Matt Dillon. German composer Englebert Humperdinck and crooner Englebert Humperdinck. Comedian Billy Crystal and conservative publisher William Kristol. Hollywood composer Alfred Newman and *Mad* magazine mascot Alfred E. Neuman. *Laugh-In* comedian Henry Gibson and Norwegian playwright Henrik Ibsen.

But the most pyrotechnic same-name pairing of all is opera giant Giuseppe Verdi and the translation of his name from Italian into English—Pittsburgh Steelers lineman "Mean" Joe Greene.

Pen-Ultimate Names

Pen names are masks that allow us to unmask ourselves.

—TERRI GUILLMETS

The authors of *Alice's Adventures in Wonderland, Silas Marner,* and *Nineteen Eighty-Four* have something in common besides being British. They are all better known by their pseudonyms, or pen names, than by their real names.

It's hard to imagine why a writer who goes to the trouble of scratching out a work of art would want to be known by another identity. On the other hand, if you were born Amantine Lucile Aurore Dupin, Anatole-François Thibault, or Aleksey Maximovich Peshkov, you might adopt the nom de plume of George Sand, Anatole France, or Maxim Gorky. And, if it's efficiency you seek, it's obvious that Moliere, Voltaire, and Stendhal are considerably more compact than Jean-Baptiste Poquelin, François-Marie Arouet, and Marie-Henri Beyle.

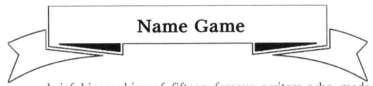

Name Game

Here are brief biographies of fifteen famous writers who made the change. From the information supplied, identify each pseudonym:

1. Eric Arthur Blair wrote a long fable about a society in which some animals are more equal than others. In 1948 he published a novel about a nightmarish society of the future, one in which everybody had a Big Brother.

2. Samuel Langhorne Clemens was a steamboat pilot before he became a writer. In 1863 he took on the pen name that was a nostalgic reminder of his riverboat days.

3. In March 1836, what has been described as the most successful writing career in history was launched with the publication of *The Posthumous Papers of the Pickwick Club.* The author, of course, was Charles Dickens. In 1833, when he was only twenty-one, Dickens began contributing stories and essays to magazines and published them pseudonymously in a collection called *Sketches by* _____.

4. Charles Lutwidge Dodgson was fascinated with words, logic, and little girls. Out of these interests he fashioned a wonderland of characters—Alice, the White Rabbit, Humpty Dumpty, the Jabberwock, the Mad Hatter, and the Red Queen.

5. Famous for her novels describing life in nineteenth century England, including *Adam Bede, Silas Marner,* and *Middlemarch,* Mary Ann Evans adopted a masculine pen name, by George.

6. He meant what he said, and he said what he meant, and his books have pleased children one hundred percent. Theodore Geisel conjured up and drew a Grinch, a Lorax, and a Cat in the Hat that now exist in the imaginations of generations of children.

7. Convicted of embezzlement, William Sydney Porter spent almost four years in prison, where he began his career as an immensely popular writer of short stories. Most of his tales are about life in New York and are marked by surprise endings.

8. Late in life, after a long career as a veterinary surgeon, James Alfred Wight began writing books that communicated his profound affection for animals. The titles of four of those books are taken from a hymn that begins, "All things bright and beautiful, all creatures great and small."

9. Jozef Korzeniowski was born in Poland and grew up speaking no English until he was seventeen, yet he became one of the greatest stylists ever to use the English language. A sailor as a youth, Korzeniowski is most famous for his stories and novels of the sea.

10. Hector Hugh Munro was killed in action during World War I. He left behind him the charming, often biting short stories to which he signed a pseudonym borrowed from *The Rubaiyat.*

11. An unpublished Atlanta writer named Peggy Marsh submitted an incomplete manuscript that filled a large suitcase. The title of the novel was to be *Tomorrow Is Another Day,* and its heroine was to be called Pansy. After a great number of changes, including the title and name of the heroine, the book was published in 1936 and quickly became an all-time bestseller, inspiring a blockbuster movie.

12. Russian-born Yiddish author Solomon Rabinovich took his pen name from a Hebrew expression meaning "peace be unto you."

13. British novelist and critic John A. B. Wilson is most famous for *A Clockwork Orange.* His works often combine word play and a grim view of life.

14. Baroness Karen Blixen, a Danish author who wrote primarily in English, managed a coffee plantation in British East Africa. She is best known for her tales and autobiography drawn from her African experiences.

15. For many years, Emanuel Benjamin Lepofski and his cousin Daniel Nathan functioned as one author, an eccentric bookworm who allegedly wrote about his adventures as a detective.

Answers

1. George Orwell 2. Mark Twain 3. Boz 4. Lewis Carroll 5. George Eliot

6. Dr. Seuss 7. O. Henry 8. James Herriot 9. Joseph Conrad 10. Saki

11. Margaret Mitchell 12. Sholem Aleichem 13. Anthony Burgess 14. Isak Dinesen 15. Ellery Queen

***

On a February day in 1892, Charles Buzelle, who had lain unconscious for nine days without food and water, was virtually DOA by the time he got to St. Vincent's Hospital. Doctors battled the odds to keep him alive—and won. The heroism of the medical staff so impressed Buzelle's married sister that when she gave birth to a daughter not long thereafter, she honored the institution by making it part of the baby's name. That's how poet Edna St. Vincent Millay came to be named—in dactylic trimeter!—for a New York hospital.

Edna St. Vincent Millay is a trinomial, that is, a person who is best known by three names. How many trinomials do you hear or read about in today's news? Sure, a handful of triple names come to mind—Andrew Lloyd Webber, Neil Patrick Harris, Sandra Day O'Connor, Ruth Bader Ginsburg, Joyce Carol Oates, and Mary Higgins Clark. But this small band of exceptions reminds us of an age gone by when to be known by three names was nothing out of the ordinary.

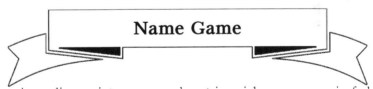

Name Game

To gain a glimpse into an age when trinomials were more in fashion, have a look at the middle names of dead poets and other writers who were best known by three names. Identify the first and last names of each writer:

1. ____ Allan ____		21. ____ Lawrence ____	
2. ____ Anne ____		22. ____ Louis ____	
3. ____ Arlington ____		23. ____ Makepeace ____	
4. ____ Barrett ____		24. ____ Maria ____	
5. ____ Bashevis ____		25. ____ May ____	
6. ____ Beecher ____		26. ____ Neale ____	
7. ____ Bernard ____		27. ____ Orne ____	

8. _____ Boothe _____		28. _____ Penn _____	
9. _____ Butler _____		29. _____ Rice _____	
10. _____ Bysshe _____		30. _____ Russell _____	
11. _____ Carlos _____		31. _____ Stanley _____	
12. _____ Chandler _____		32. _____ Taylor _____	
13. _____ Christian _____		33. _____ Vincent _____	
14. _____ Clarke _____		34. _____ Wadsworth _____	
15. _____ Conan _____		35. _____ Waldo _____	
16. _____ David _____		36. _____ Ward _____	
17. _____ Fenimore _____		37. _____ Weldon _____	
18. _____ Greenleaf _____		38. _____ Wendell _____	
19. _____ Ingalls _____		39. _____ Whitcomb _____	
20. _____ Kinnan _____		40. _____ Wollstonecraft _____	

Answers

1. Edgar Allan Poe 2. Katherine Anne Porter 3. Edwin Arlington Robinson 4. Elizabeth Barrett Browning 5. Isaac Bashevis Singer

6. Harriet Beecher Stowe 7. George Bernard Shaw 8. Clare Boothe Luce 9. William Butler Yeats 10. Percy Bysshe Shelley

11. William Carlos Williams 12. Joel Chandler Harris 13. Hans Christian Andersen 14. Clement Clarke Moore 15. Arthur Conan Doyle

16. Henry Davis Thoreau 17. James Fenimore Cooper 18. John Greenleaf Whittier 19. Laura Ingalls Wilder 20. Marjorie Kinnan Rawlings

21. Ernest Lawrence Thayer 22. Robert Louis Stevenson 23. William Makepeace Thackeray 24. Erich Maria Remarque 25. Louisa May Alcott

26. Zora Neale Hurston 27. Sarah Orne Jewett 28. Robert Penn Warren 29. Edgar Rice Burroughs 30. James Russell Lowell

31. Erle Stanley Gardner 32. Samuel Taylor Coleridge 33. Stephen Vincent Benét 34. Henry Wadsworth Longfellow 35. Ralph Waldo Emerson

36. Julia Ward Howe or Henry Ward Beecher 37. James Weldon Johnson 38. Oliver Wendell Holmes 39. James Whitcomb Riley 40. Mary Wollstonecraft Shelley

THE LIGHTER SIDE
OF NAMES

Names at Play

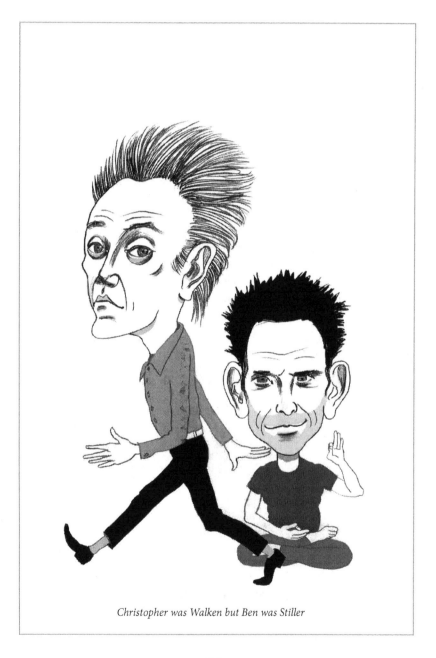

Christopher was Walken but Ben was Stiller

What do you call a man hanging on your wall? *Art.* A man stretched out on your front porch? *Matt.* A man who's fallen into a pile of leaves? *Russell.* A man used as fishing bait? *Bob.* A man who's fallen into a toilet? *John* or *Lou.* A man ground into hamburger? *Chuck* or *Mac.* A man who's buried? *Doug.* A man passed out in a rice field? *Paddy.* A man stuffed into a hole? *Phil.* A man stuffed into a hot dog bun? *Frank.* A man stuffed into a mailbox? *Bill.* A man stuffed into a car trunk? *Jack.* A man stuffed into a rabbit burrow? *Warren.* A man covered with cat scratches? *Claude.* A man who's a hypochondriac? *Isaac.* A man who's the sucker at the poker table? *Mark.* An oversexed man? *Randy.* Two men hanging on your window? *Curt 'n' Rod.*

What do you call a woman who throws her shopping bills into the fire? *Bernadette.* A woman with a wooden leg? *Peg.* A one-legged woman? *Eileen.* A one-legged Japanese woman? *Irene.* A Chinese woman caught in a food mixer? *Brenda.* A woman who wears cheap pant suits? *Polly Esther.* A woman stuck in an ancient lamp? *Jeannie.* A woman trapped in a church tower? *Belle.* A crazy woman? *Dotty.* A woman with a bloodshot eye? *Iris.* A woman who's fallen down a rabbit hole. *Bunny.* A conceited woman? *Mimi.* A woman who won't stop talking? *Gabby.* A woman who complains a lot? *Mona.* A woman with a loud voice? *Blair.*

What do you call a man who can't stand up? *Neil.* A Mexican with a rubber digit? *Roberto.* A man who is water skiing? *Skip.* A man who is accident prone? *Rex.* A man who got struck by lightning? *Smoky.* A man who got hit by a truck? *Van.* A man who fell into boiling water? *Stu.* A man who cut himself shaving? *Nick.* A man who broke a tooth? *Chip.* A man who fell off a mountain? *Cliff* or *Craig.* A man with keys and a lisp? *Keith.* A man in pain with a lisp? *Thor.* A man deep in debt? *Owen.* A man crying his eyes out? *Waylon.* A man with a knife in his stomach? *Pierce.* A man who's expired? *Barry.* A man who's buried in a junkyard? *Rusty.* A man crushed by construction machinery? *Derrick.* And a man who smells like a cow? *Barney.*

What do you call a woman covered with multiple stings? *Bea.* A woman cut by wire? *Barb.* A woman hit by a truck? *Lorrie.* A woman who fell into a swamp? *Marsha.* A woman who fell into boiling water? *Blanche.* A woman who fell out of an airplane? *Ariel.* A woman burnt by a grill? *Barbie* or *Char.* A woman ground up into hamburger? *Patty.* A woman with a big bottom? *Fanny.* A woman caught in a hurricane? *Gail.* A woman who's been swindled? *Patsy.* A woman who's expired? *Di.* A woman buried in the desert? *Sandy.* A woman who's fallen into a toilet? *Flo.* And a woman who's fallen into two toilets? *Lulu.*

Okay, those were a tad nasty but, I hope, a tad funny, too. Now enjoy some safer name play:

Have you heard about the thief who burgled an art museum but didn't have enough fuel in his engine to escape the police? Apparently, the criminal didn't have enough Monet to buy Degas to fill Lautrec and make the van Gogh.

Who was the law-breaking friar? His name was Felonious Monk. The aquatic scientist-janitor? Jacques Custodian.

Add to the assemblage the two dyspeptic lawmen—Wild Bill Hiccup and Wyatt Burp. What do Peter the Great, Richard the Lionhearted, Cedric the Entertainer, and Winnie the Pooh have in common? They all have the same middle name—*The.*

And what happened when Napoleon Bonaparte threw a grenade into a recreation room? The result was linoleum blown apart.

Senior citizens are surrounded by a lot of friends: As soon as they wake up, Will Power is there to help them get out of bed. Then they go visit John. When they play golf, Charley Horse shows up to be their partner. As soon as Charley leaves, along come Arthur Ritis and his five aunts—Aunt Acid, Auntie Oxidant, Auntie Biotic, Auntie Coagulant, and Auntie Inflammatory—and they go the rest of the day from joint to joint. After such a busy day, they're Petered and Tuckered out and glad to go to bed—with Ben Gay, of course!

It wasn't that long ago that Steve Jobs, Johnny Cash, and Bob Hope were alive. But now we have no Jobs, no Cash, and no Hope.

It's so much fun to move names out of their usual hangars and make them soar heavenward, up to the Sun Yat-Sen, Warren Moon, Ringo Starr, Freddie Mercury, Venus Williams, and Bruno Mars:

- Oscar was Wilde, but Thornton was Wilder.
- Dame May was Whitty, but John Greenleaf was Whittier.
- Anne was Frank and Emily Blunt.
- Eddie will Cantor, but George will Gallup.
- Ellen was Burstyn, but R. Buckminster was Fuller.
- Dwight was Moody, but Tavis was Smiley.
- James was Reston, but Herman Wouk.
- Claire Boothe broke Luce, and Morgan was a Freeman.
- Christopher was Walken and Alan Turing, but Ben was Stiller.

- Will was Ferrell, Michael Savage, and Amy Madigan.

- Timothy was Leary and Stevie did Wonder, but Lady was Gaga.

- Frank was Loesser, but Julianne Moore, Johnny Most, and George Best.

- Tim was Tiny, Rich Little, and Martin Short, but Huey was Long and Henry Wadsworth was a Longfellow.

- Lionel was Messi, Luther Strange, Kevin Spacey, Wallace Beery, Robin Thicke, Maria Callas, and Howard Stern.

- Christopher was Smart, Madeleine Albright, Stephen Wright, and James Worthy.

- I've seen Courtney Love and Richard Loving, but Jane was Fonda.

- Tim hated Raines, Phileas Fogg, Robert Frost, C. P. Snow, Crystal Gayle, and Roger Mudd, while Floyd loved Mayweather.

- William Hurt, Tom was in Paine, John did Wayne, Roger Ailes, and Merle is Haggard, but Lance is Armstrong, Blake Lively, Nathan Hale, and Thomas Hardy.

- Schecky was Greene, Barry White, James Brown, Joel Gray, Arthur Ashe, Vida Blue, Lewis Black, Harry Golden, Amy Tan (but Roscoe Tanner), Pete Rose, Will Scarlett, Stephen Pinker, and Gloria Allred.

- Larry Speakes and William will Tell, but Janet was Yellen, Ellen Barkin, and Saul will Bellow.

- Robert was Young, Henny a Youngman, and Tank Younger, but Victor was Mature, Gary an Oldman, and Paul a Newman.

- Tom was Petty, Noah Wylie, James Randi, Ray a Kroc, and Noel a Coward, but Harry was a Truman, Benny a Goodman, Ivan the Reitman, Bob a Corker, Joseph Priestley, Andy Devine, and Alfred Nobel.

- Robert was Downey, Albert Finney, Edmund Muskie (exuding Elon Musk), Al Kaline alkaline, and Terry Gross, but Ricky was Fowler and Mark Spitz.

- John Crow Ransom, Taylor was Swift, and Howard Fast. Watch Vincent van Gogh, Geoffrey Rush, and Usain Bolt.

- Oliver can Twist, Chris Rock, and Norman Rockwell.

- Tom will DeLay, Leslie Stahl, and Karl Rove, but Frederick will March, Helen Hunt, Chevy Chase, and Geoffrey Rush.

- Buddy will Hackett, Steve Wynn, and Donald Trump.

- Immanuel Kant but Theresa May, George Will, and Anne Hathaway.

And for sports lovers:

- In the baseball game, Henry was Fielding and also hit a Homer.

- In basketball, John Fowles, but referee Erskine Caldwell.

- In football, Robert will Bloch while Huey goes Long and John throws Dos Passos.

- In skiing. Jeff Flake, Robert Frost, and Phoebe Snow will whiz down the Grant Hill.

- In sculling, Nicholas will Rowe, Tom will Cruise, and George will handle the Orwell.

- In racing, the Walter de la Mare won the derby in a George Gallup.

- At the rodeo, Pearl will Buck, but Sally will Ride the Jason Bull.

- In golf, Minnie's Driver put the Lonzo Ball right on the Graham Greene while Humphrey shot a Bogie but Jack shot Parr.

- In tennis, Tennis E. Williams and Alfred, Lord Tennis Son write about the unreturnable Robert W. Service.

Indubitably—and take it from me, voted International Punster of the Year—names are made to be played with, and that's just what we'll be doing in the rest of *The Joy of Names*.

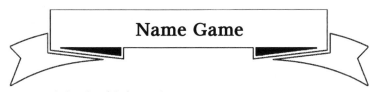

Name Game

Connect each book with its author:

by

1.	*Animal Diseases*	Anita Job
2.	*Archery Made Easy*	Ann Thrax
3.	*Arctic Weather*	Bill Jerome Home
4.	*Bartending Made Easy*	Bowen Arrow
5.	*The French Chef*	Dinah Sore
6.	*Handel's Messiah*	Fay Slift
7.	*House Construction*	Fillmore Glasses
8.	*How to Find Work*	Frazier Bunsoff
9.	*How to Say No*	Halsey Monty Zuma
10.	*It's Springtime!*	Hammond Cheese
11.	*Looking Younger*	Howard I. Know

12. *My Pants Fell Down*   Jim Nasium
13. *Neither a Borrower*   Kurt Reply
14. *Popular Sandwiches*   Lucy Lastic
15. *Prehistoric Reptiles*   Nora Lender Bee
16. *Sherlock Does It Again*   Ollie Luyah
17. *Traveling Around the Globe* Scott Linyard
18. *Was O. J. Guilty?*   Sue Flay
19. *Working Out*   Treesa Green
20. *World War II Battles*   Wanda Lust

Answers

1. Ann Thrax 2. Bowen Arrow 3. Frazier Bunsoff 4. Fillmore Glasses 5. Sue Flay

6. Ollie Luyah 7. Bill Jerome Home 8. Anita Job 9. Kurt Reply 10. Treesa Green

11. Fay Slift 12. Lucy Lastic 13. Nora Lender Bee 14. Hammond Cheese 15. Dinah Sore

16. Scott Linyard 17. Wanda Lust 18. Howard I. Know 19. Jim Nasium 20. Halsey Monty Zuma

Funny Business

Dewey, Cheatem & Howe

C alvin Coolidge, the thirtieth president of the United States, once proclaimed, "The business of America is business." Business is also the business of name play.

The wildly popular public radio show "Car Talk" stamped into the national psyche the law firm of Dewey, Cheatem & Howe.

Along those lines, have you heard about the authors Anne Thology, Bess Cellar, Mel O'Drama, Page Turner, Rita Book, and Warren Peace?

Have you heard about the musicians Bertha D. Blues, Bessie Mae Mucho, Midas Welby Spring, Clara Nett, Phil Harmonic, Vic Trola, Melody Lingerzon, and Walt Stime? Have you heard about the composer who wrote a song for his ex-wives?: "Don't Cry for Me, Marge and Tina."

Have you heard about the dentists Dee Kay, Flossy Teeth, Hal Itosis, and Hopalong Cavity? Have you heard about the sporting goods salesmen Dennis Ball, Chip Shot, and Clarence Sale?

Have you heard about the automobile distributors C. Everett Coupe, Denton Fender, LaToyota Jackson, Manuel Transmission, Mick Jaguar, Morrie Missions, Oscar de la Rental, Richard Gear, Warren T. Muffler, and Stu D. Baker?

Have you heard about the transportation specialists Sally Forth, Otto Bonn, Rhoda Boat, Orson Buggy, Lisa Carr, T. Rollie Carr, Cher D. Rhodes, Cara Vann, Mandy Lifeboats, Rick Shaw, R. R. Twain, and Dee Tour?

Have you heard about the veterinarians Ali Katz, Charlie Horse, Don Key, Ella Funt, Lovey Dove, Q. T. Puppy, and Ted E. Behr?

Have you heard about the Bible enthusiasts Jenna Sis, Adam Zapple, Noah Zark, Pearl E. Gates, Rev. Elation, Gloria N. Excelsis, Holly Luya, Judith Priest, and Faith Healer?

Have you heard about the chefs Al Dente, Alan Greasepan, Artie Choke, Barbie Q. Sauce, Candide Yam, Cole Slaw, Dee Licious, Della Catessen, Karen Feeding, Newt Tritious, Ann Chovy, Marsha Mellow, Ham Berger, Mutton Jeff, Sue Flay, Lynne Gweeny, Graham K. Racker, S. Irving Spoon, and Sal Addressing?

Have you heard about the con artists Robin Steele, Jimmy DeLocke, Armand A. Legg, Count R. Fitz, and Hank E. Panky?

Have you heard about the physicians Collier Doctor, Penny Cillin, Thor Throat, Willa Catheter, and Winston Payne?

Have you heard about the psychotherapists Lois Steem, Ed G. Ness, Ophelia Paine, Cody Pendant, Mel N. Collie, Izzy Crazy, Faith Healer, Sheila Just, Hank R. Schiff, Molly Coddle, Rudy Day, Sarah Bellum, Whit

Send, and Zane Asylum?

And have you heard about the cross-country travel guides Al Abama, Al Aska, Alan Arkin Saw, Ari Zona, Cal Ifornia, Carol Lina, Dakota Fanning, Della Ware, Flora Duh, Georgia O'Keefe, Ida Ho, Ken Tucky, Louise E. Anna, Mary Land, Minnie Sota, Miss Ouri, Mrs. Sippi, Joe Montana, Tennessee Williams, and Virginia Woolf?

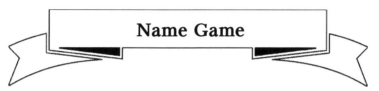

Name Game

Match each job with a funny name, as in "manicurist = Emory Board":

1.	astrologer	Barb Dwyer
2.	audiologist	Barbara Seville
3.	chromosome researcher	Barbie Dahl
4.	college administrator	Cher Cropper
5.	computer specialist	Claire Voyant
6.	dentist	Cy Burnett
7.	earring seller	Deena Students
8.	electrician	Esther Bonnet
9.	farm supplies seller	Gene Poole
10.	farmer	Ginger Vitis
11.	judo instructor	Horace Cope
12.	justice of the peace	Jenna Rater
13.	lawyer	Jerry Atric
14.	lumberjack	Jerry Mander
15.	medium	Judy Ism
16.	milliner	Laura Biden
17.	newspaper editor	Lou Pole
18.	opera singer	Louden Clear
19.	police officer	Marcus Fair
20.	politician	Marion A. Chapel
21.	rabbi	Marshall Artz
22.	rest home nurse	Phil E. Buster
23.	senator	Pierce Deers
24.	teacher	Tab Lloyd
25.	toy seller	Tim Burr

Answers

1. Horace Cope 2. Louden Clear 3. Gene Poole 4. Deena Students 5. Cy Burnett

6. Ginger Vitis 7. Pierce Deers 8. Jenna Rater 9. Barb Dwyer 10. Cher Cropper 11. Marshall Artz 12. Marion A. Chapel 13. Lou Pole 14. Tim Burr 15. Claire Voyant

16. Esther Bonnet 17. Tab Lloyd 18. Barbara Seville 19. Laura Biden 20. Jerry Mander

21. Judy Ism 22. Jerry Atric 23. Phil E. Buster 24. Marcus Fair 25. Barbie Dahl

Incorrigible punster that I am (don't incorrige me!), I have noticed that some words start with something that sounds like a first name and then comes a patronymic *O'*. So have you heard about these thirty famous Irish men and women?:

- the Irish botanist Phil O'Dendron;
- the Irish heart surgeon Angie O' Plasty;
- the Irish theater owner Nick O'Lodeon;
- the Irish cigarette manufacturer Nick O'Teen;
- the Irish watchmaker Nick O'Time;
- the Irish marksman Rick O'Shay;
- the Irish barber Hank O'Hare;
- the Irish con artist Upton O'Goode;
- the Irish musician Vi O'Lynn;
- the Irish puppeteer Mary O'Nette;
- the Irish meteorologist Barry O'Metric;
- the Irish inventor of Halloween Jack O'Lantern;
- the Irish manufacturer of flooring Lynn O'Leum;
- the Irish printer Mimi O'Graph;
- the Irish playwright Mel O'Drama;
- the Irish poet Ann O'Nymous;
- the Irish gum specialist Perry O'Dontal;
- the Irish tracer of ancestors Jeannie O'Logical;
- the Irish singer Carrie O'Key;

- the Irish pasta chef Ravi O'Lee;
- the Irish sportsman Mark O'Polo;
- the Irish ornithologist Bob O'Link;
- the Irish vegetable grower Brock O'Lee;
- the Irish entomologist Chris O'Liss;
- the Irish druggist Ben O'Drill;
- the Irish shipper Bill O'Lading;
- the Irish funeral speaker Yul O'Gee;
- the Irish cancer researcher Carson O'Genic;
- the Irish poison manufacturer Cy O'Nide;
- and the Irish designer for outdoor living Patty O'Furniture!

Names as Nouns

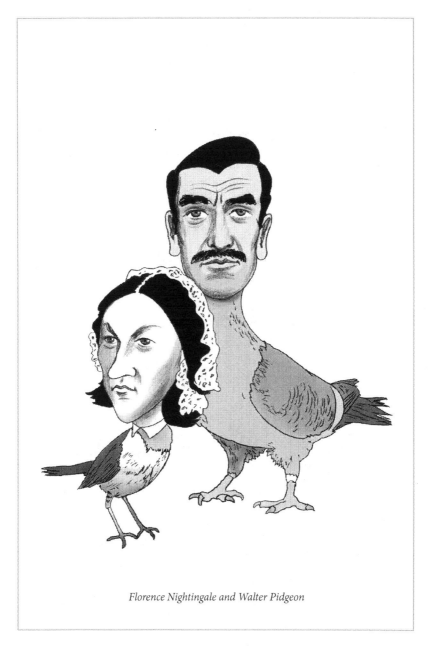

Florence Nightingale and Walter Pidgeon

Do you remember back in junior high and high school when you were taught that a noun was a person, place, or thing? But you probably didn't learn that names can be nouns, as the following narrative demonstrates:

Welcome to our fair city. We invite you to take one of our scenic tours. All tours include regular stops at clean restrooms, featuring the Leslie Stahl, Elton John, Lucy Liu, and Thomas Crapper.

Our botanical tour goes east into our Ted Forrest. It's primarily Chris Pine, but your guide will point out the Lefty Grove of Marla Maples, a John Birch, a Joey Chestnut, and a Nathaniel Hawthorne. With fall approaching, you may see a gold Ryan Leaf or two.

You'll continue through the Clint Eastwood, which features Austin Hedges, two George Bushes, and a lot of Buddy Holly, Phil Ivy, and Ellsworth Vines.

You'll have time for a short walk along some Dusty Rhodes in the Sally Field. You are allowed to pick the Gennifer Flowers in Claire Bloom in the Gunter Grass so that you can fashion your own Judy Garland. But avoid the Graig Nettles. They sting.

Our second tour is of our unique zoo on Picabo Street. All the exhibits are artfully arranged around beautiful Lily Pons.

Start with the Brian Grazers—John Deere, including a Pearl Buck and John Doe, a Jason Bull, Sandra Bullock, Crazy Horse, Walter de la Mare, and her Nick Foles enclosed in the Sean Penn.

Move on to the carnivores—the Leonard Lyons and a Dick Tiger, Max Bear, Peter Coyote, John Cougar, Jamie Foxx, and Tom Wolfe.

The stars of our primate mesa are the Edward Gibbon, Barbara Mandrell, and Thelonious Monk.

The Julia Child's section features an Elizabeth Warren teeming with bunnies and William Burroughs crammed with prairie dogs. The kiddies will also enjoy the petting corral, which encloses Katz and a Snoop Dogg, Charles Lamb, Captain Kangaroo, and Jason Kidd. The zookeepers protect your children by from time to time picking a Gomer Pyle of Billy Crudup.

Next proceed to the Larry Bird Exhibit. In the Nicolas Cage you'll have a Clarence Birdseye view of Tim Robbins, along with a Stephen Crane, Rita Dove, Jenny Finch, Ryan Gosling, John Jay, Dean Martin, Florence Nightingale, Walter Pidgeon, Dan Quayle, Jack Sparrow, Lynn Swann, Taylor Swift, and Christopher Wren, all living together and flying freely. As with the large mammals, predators such as the Tony Hawk, Sheryl Crow, Tom Kite, and Andrea Jaeger are housed separately.

Also on our Franz Liszt of tours is a trip north up Jonah Hill and down Alan-a-Dale to see the geological features of our area. Traversing an Alan Greenspan, you'll pass the Hugh Downs, John Glenn, Brandon Heath, Jayne Meadows, Red Grange with its Marvin Barnes, and through the Beyoncé Knowles, where you'll stop for a short walk on the Michael Moore.

On to Rick Mount, where you'll travel along the Matthew Ridgway to the Pat Summitt. There you'll see the Chris Rock and the Emma Stone balanced on the edge of the Jimmy Cliff. The Cecil Rhodes will dip down through the Steve Canyon to the Frankie Valli, where you'll visit archaeological digs at the William Tell and the Brad Pitt. As you cross the Jeff Bridges, you can look up at the spectacular panorama of the Daniel Craig.

In our fourth tour you get to view our local Muddy Waters. You'll pass through some Karl–Anthony Townes to reach the Henry Cabot Lodge and Walter Camp on the west side of the Tyra Banks of Veronica Lake, a reservoir created by the Jean-Claude Van Damme. Traveling downstream along the Cliff Branch of the Joan Rivers, you'll see it widen into the Wade Boggs and Ngaio Marsh. A Nelson Eddy has created a Donna Reed-choked Deadpool, in which you won't want to Dwayne Wade. Farther downstream, the river empties into the Justin Timberlake.

When you view the Ethel Waters emptying into the Danny Ocean, you will watch the roaring Ryan Seacrest. The Mel Brooks empty into the Michael Bay, where a large colony of Bobby Seale enjoys the abundant food supply of Buster Crabbe, Hamilton Fish, Theodore Sturgeon, and Newton B. Minnow. You may want to walk across the Lorna Doone on the George Sand of the Michael Beach to see them. At the Dinah Shore you'll walk along the Dick Van Dyke, but watch out for the Bennett Cerf. At high tide, it can be dangerous.

All our tours end with a pass through our downtown, built around the Aubrey Plaza. You'll start on Della Street, where you'll see the Jude Law center, Margaret Court house and the Frank Church. Note the John Tower that features an Alexander Graham Bell and which is topped by a Christopher Cross of Jamie Gold. Next to the church and behind the John Wall is our historic cemetery. You can return later to visit the Robert Graves of our early settlers. The Henry Louis Gates are on the side facing the church.

You'll then pass the Sheldon Whitehouse. Don't miss the ornate Clark Gable facing the street. Next up, the Hayley Mills, now a museum. There you'll be able to visit our Jewel exhibit, which includes the Billy Crystal, Neil Diamond, Kevin Garnett, Minnie Pearl, Jack Ruby, and William

Safire. Featured are two famous bejeweled game pieces, the Fats Domino and Chubby Checker, vivid against the Jane Curtain backdrop. These valuable items are kept under John Locke and Francis Scott Key.

There's also a clothing exhibition in the Arsenio Hall. Among the featured items are the Red Buttons, Mickey Mantle, Ben Coates, Al Capp, Roy Acuff, Elisabeth Shue, Goody Two-Shoes, Jack Sock, Pippi Longstocking, Will Shortz, and Desmond Tutu, woven from a Christian Bale of Joseph Cotton.

Across the Kirstie Alley, you'll see the Orson Welles, formerly the source of the town water supply. Complete the circuit of the commercial area by passing the Emily Post office, the Shirley Temple, the Amy Winehouse, and the Rosanne Barr.

The last stop on your Linda Tripp will be to the Rosa Parks, where you will sample delicious, fresh food at the farmers' market, including a Halle Berry, Don Cherry, Gilbert Grape, Jack Lemmon, Milt Plum, Darryl Strawberry, Billy Beane, Dom Capers, Willie Mays, Ty Cobb of David Corn, Joyce Carol Oates, and Anne Rice. You can take away a Gregory Peck of Julius Peppers.

I'm confident that the Alan Turing of our great city will make your Billie Holiday the Pete Best, and never the Ralph Nader, of your life, but you be the Aaron Judge of that.

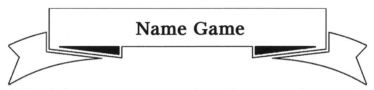

Name Game

As well as being nouns, names can be verbs, a part of speech that expresses action. Have you seen, for example, Paul Manafort ("man a fort") and Paula Poundstone ("pound stone")?

Match each real-life first name with each real-life last name.

Have you seen . . .?

1.	Al	Buffett
2.	Alonzo	Carrey
3.	Bob	Carroll
4.	Dakota	Cooke
5.	Diahann	Cruise
6.	Diana	Danson
7.	Donald	Fanning

8. Enos	Fetchit
9. Franklin	Ford
10. Gerald	Garner
11. Harriet Beecher	Gore
12. Harvey	Harden
13. James	Hope
14. Jane	Lear
15. Jennifer	Milk
16. Jim	Mourning
17. Norman	Pickett
18. Paul	Pierce
19. Sally	Revere
20. Sam	Ride
21. Stepin	Rigg
22. Ted	Russell
23. Tom	Slaughter
24. Warren	Stowe
25. Wilson	Trump

Answers

1. Al Gore 2. Alonzo Mourning 3. Bob Hope 4. Dakota Fanning 5. Diahnn Carroll

6. Diana Rigg 7. Donald Trump 8. Enos Slaughter 9. Franklin Pierce 10. Gerald Ford

11. Harriet Beecher Stowe 12. Harvey Milk 13. James Harden 14. Jane Russell 15. Jennifer Garner

16. Jim Carrey 17. Norman Lear 18. Paul Revere 19. Sally Ride 20. Sam Cooke

21. Stepin Fetchit 22. Ted Danson 23. Tom Cruise 24. Warren Buffett 25 Wilson Pickett.

When Names Collide

Santa Claustrophobia

- If Al Franken campaigned for president with Jill Stein as his running mate, they'd be called the Franken Stein ticket.
- If Natalie Portman dressed to the nines, she'd be Natalie attired.
- If you attend an Edith Piaf concert where pastry is served for dessert, you can have your cake and Edith, too.
- If a TV host wrote a book about atheism, he'd be called Author Godfrey.
- If elephants could sing, the best of them would be Harry Elephante and Elephant Gerald.
- If the New York Yankees had traded away Babe Ruth, they would have become Ruthless.
- If Al Gore dexterously danced the Macarena, he would have demonstrated Al Gore rhythm.
- If Vladimir Putin parachuted onto the roof of a fancy hotel, he'd be Putin on the Ritz.
- If you have no coins to insert for the pay toilet, you out of Johnny Cash.
- If Yo Yo Ma received an M.A. in Music, he'd be Yo Yo Ma M.A.
- If J. K. Rowling rolls, Stephen Hawking hawks, Debra Messing messes, Ted Tingling tingles, Alonzo Mourning mourns, and Dakota Fanning fans, then Rudyard Kipling kipples.
- If you cross a gorilla with a ceramics worker, you get a Harry Potter.
- If you cross a gorilla with the computer Watson, you get a Harry Reasoner.
- If you cross a trumpeter with an auto mechanic, you get Toot and Car Man.
- If Walt Whitman published an anthology of his poetry, it would be called the Whitman Sampler.
- If you stick a feather in Al Capp, you'll call it Mickey Rooney.
- If Guinevere gave Lancelot, I wonder how much Galahad.
- If Charles Dickens ordered a martini, it comes with an Olive or Twist.
- If Saint Nicholas has a fear of getting stuck in a chimney, he suffers from Santa Claustrophobia.
- If Fannie Farmer produced a box of candy for cannibals, it would be filled with Farmer's Fannies.

- If Freda Kahlo ran a stable, it would be called Freda Livery.

- If Gloria Estefan fell ill while driving her car at the beginning of the week, she'd be *sic transit Gloria mundi!*

It's even more fun to play with multiple mergers and founders. For example, if the BBC, Internet, and Yahoo ever merged, the new corporation would be named BB Net and Yahoo. So let's have a look at these start-up companies:

- If Cy Young and Björn Borg started a business together, it would be called Cy Borg.

- If Clay Aiken and Walter Pidgeon started a business together, it would be called Clay Pidgeon.

- If Darryl Strawberry and Billy Sunday started a business together, it would be called Strawberry Sunday,

- If Salvador Dali and Fernando Lamas started a business together, it would be called Dali Lamas.

- If Tori Spelling and Samantha Bee started a business together, it would be called Spelling Bee.

- If Johnny Cash and Mariah Carey started a business together, it would be called Cash and Carey.

- If Iggy Pop and David Korn started a business together, it would be called Pop Korn.

- If Lyle Lovett, Bobby Orr, and Mike Leavitt started a business together, it would be called Lovett Orr Leavitt.

- If Franz Joseph Haydn and Zeke Elliott started a business together, it would be called Haydn Zeke.

- If Schecky Green and Terrence Stamp started a business together, it would be called Green Stamp.

- If Charlize Theron, Vanessa Angel, and Heather Angel started a business together, it would be called Charlize Angels.

- If Walter Winchell and Max Factor started a business together, it would be called Winchell Factor.

- If Tai Babilonia, Michele Kwan, and John Doe started a business together, it would be called Tai Kwan Doe.

- If Liv Tyler, Howie Long, and William Shakespeare's Prospero started a business together, it would be called Liv Long and Prospero.

- If Otto Graham, Mo Rocca, and Jennifer Beals started a business together, it would be called Otto Mo Beals.

- If Sadaharu Oh, Jack Lord, Sandra Dee, and Marjorie Lord started a business together, it would be called Oh Lord Dee Lord.

- If Jeffrey Tambor, Draymond Green, and Thomas Mann started a business together, it would be called Tambor Green Mann.

- If Alex Trebek, Sander Vanocur, Jon Hamm, and John Milton started a business together, it would be called Alex Sander Hamm Milton.

- If Gwen Ifill, John Tower, Paris Hilton, and Dennis Franz started a business together, it would be called Ifill Tower Paris Franz.

- If Don King and Don Knotts started a business together, it would be called Don King Don Knotts.

- If Snoop Dogg and Winnie the Pooh started a business together, it would be called Snoop Dogg Pooh.

- If Anna Kendrick, David Merrick, James Caan, and Fannie Flagg started a business together, it would be called Anna Merrick Caan Flagg.

- If Mia Hamm, Maya Angelou, and Lamont Cranston started a business together, it would be called Mia and Maya Shadow.

- If Nathan Hale, Mary Poppins, R. Buckminster Fuller, and Grace Kelly started a business together, it would be called Hale Mary Fuller Grace.

- If W. C. Handy, Al Capp, Jack Paar, and Stephen King started a business together, it would be called Handy Capp Paar King.

- If Woody Harrelson, Natalie Wood, Gregory Peck, and Ben Hur started a business together, it would be called Woody Wood Peck Hur.

- If Eddie Rickenbacker, Elvis Presley, Elizabeth of Great Britain, John F. Kennedy, and Bo Derek started a business together, it would be called Ace King Queen Jack Ten.

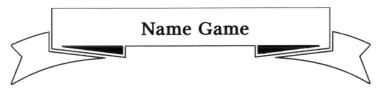

Name Game

Here are ten more business teams. What would each corporation be called?

1. Phoebe Snow and Betty White
2. Bing Crosby and Cherry Jones
3. Roger Federer and Malcolm X
4. Jack Black and Franz Liszt
5. Chip Kelly and Dale Earnhardt
6. Polly Bergen and Esther Williams
7. Gladys Knight and Doris Day
8. Donald Sterling and Adam Silver
9. baseball stars Ty Cobb and Herb Score
10. baseball stars Boog Powell and Felipe Alou

Answers

1. Snow White 2. Bing Cherry 3. Fed X 4. Black Liszt 5. Chip and Dale

6. Polly Esther 7. Knight and Day 8. Sterling Silver 9. Ty Score 10. Boog Alou

The Hello Name Game

Chick and Henny raise poultry

These days, we often attend conferences, parties, and other gatherings where we are asked to wear name tags that say, "Hello, My Name is _____." The beloved humorist Erma Bombeck tells this story: "A member of the committee slapped a name tag over my left bosom. 'What shall we name the other one?' I smiled. She was not amused."

Here's a punderful game that takes those badges to the limit. The object is to match a real first name with a real profession to spark a punny connection, as in "My name is Lorrie, and I'm a trucker," "My name is Ophelia, and I'm a masseuse," and "My name is Tyler, and I design bathrooms."

Hello, our names are . . .

• Abbott, Abby, Angel, Charity, Chastity, Christian, Faith, Glory, Grace, Hope, Mercy, Neal, and Temple, and we're servants of the church.

• Ace, Bette, Chip, and Delia, and we work in a casino.

• Alexis, Axel, Cab, Carmen, Chevy, Jack, Mercedes, Otto, Phillip, Portia, and Van, and we work on cars.

• Amber, Crystal, Goldie, Jade, Jasper, Jules, Opal, Pearl, Ring, Ruby, and Sapphire, and we're jewelers.

• Annette, Bob, Brooke, Doc, Eddie, Finn, Gil, Marina, Marlon, Piers, Rod, and Rowan, and we're fisherpeople.

• April, August, January, June, May, Summer, and Tuesday, and we make calendars.

• Art, Dot, Drew, Garrett, and Hugh, and we're painters.

• Arthur and Page, and we're writers.

• Avery, Crane, Jay, Martin, Raven, Rhea, Robin, and Wren, and we're ornithologists.

• Barney, and Timothy, and we're farmers.

• Baron, Duke, Earl, Gaylord, and King, and we're noblemen.

• Barry, Di, Doug, and Paul, and we're undertakers.

• Basil, Blanche, Eaton, Ginger, Herb, Rosemary, and Sage, and we're chefs.

• Bea, Buzz, Honey, Ladybird, Midge, and Nat, and we're entomologists.

• Belle and Isabel, and we play the carillon.

• Bertha, Spike, and Ty, and we work on a railroad.

- Bill, Buck, and Penny, and we work at the mint.
- Billy and Nanny, and we herd goats.
- Bing, Cherry, Melanie, and Peaches, and we sell fruit.
- Blossom, Bud, Dahlia, Daisy, Fern, Flora, Heather, Holly, Iris, Ivy, Jasmine, Lily, Pansy, Pete, Petunia, Posey, Rose, and Violet, and we're horticulturalists.
- Branch, Forest, Hazel, Hugh, Leif, Magnolia, Myrtle, Twiggy, and Woody, and we're arborists.
- Brandy, Margarita, Olive, and Sherry, and we're bartenders.
- Buffy, Fanny, Lena, Les, and Skip, and we're weight-loss counselors.
- Bunny and Warren, and we raise rabbits.
- Candy, Carmela, Lolly, and Sugar, and we're confectioners.
- Celeste, Jupiter, Sky, Starr, and Venus, and we're astronomers.
- Chick and Henny, and we raise poultry.
- Chuck, Frank, Ham, and Stu, and we're butchers.
- CiCi, Iris, and Seymour, we're opticians.
- Claude and Rory, and we're lion tamers.
- Cliff, Craig, and Rocky, and we're mountaineers.
- Colt and Winnie, and we train horses.
- Dale, Glen, and Heath, and we sell country real estate.
- Dawn, Dewey, Gail, Hale, Misty, Sky, Storm, and Sunny, and we're meteorologists.
- Emory, Hans, and Philo, and we're manicurists.
- Flip and Patty, and we cook hamburgers.
- Flo, John, Lou, Lulu, and Piper, and we're plumbers.
- Hank and Harry, and we're barbers.
- Harmony, Harper, Lute, Melody, and Viola, and we're musicians.
- Helmut, Lance, and Pierce, and we're knights.
- Holly and Noel, and we sell Christmas plants.
- Hunter and Lionel, and we lead safaris.
- Ira and Rich, and we're investment advisers.
- Jose and Smoky, and we're firefighters.

- Josh, Smiley, and Whit, and we're comedians.
- Kitty, Tabby, and Tom, and we raise cats.
- Lacey, Levi, Serge, and Taylor, and we sell clothing.
- Laurel, Vi, Victor, and Wynne, and we're Olympic champions.
- Michelle, Sandy, Shelly, and Wade, and we're lifeguards at the beach.
- Rex and Rusty, and we own a junkyard.
- Sue and Will, and we're lawyers.

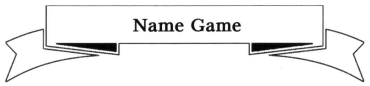

Name Game

Match each first name with his or her profession. Other answers besides the ones offered here are possible.

Hello, my name is . . .

1. Barb 2. Bart 3. Bo 4. Booker 5. Brandon 6. Brie 7. Carol 8. Carrie 9. Clay 10. Cole

11. Cookie 12. Dean 13. Derrick 14. Dick 15. Dolly 16. Dustin 17. Garrison 18. Gene 19. Grant 20. Homer

21. Jock 22. Jim 23. Jimmy 24. Joe 25. Joey 26. Lorrie 27. Manuel 28. Marcus 29. Marion 30. Marshall

31. Mason 32. Matt 33. Mike 34. Myles 35. Newt 36. Paddy 37. Pat 38. Rob 39. Russell 40. Trixie

. . . and I / I'm a(n) . . .

Answers

1. wire manufacturer 2. bus driver in San Francisco 3. archer 4. travel agent or author 5. cattle rancher 6. cheese seller 7. composer of Christmas songs 8. porter 9. potter 10. miner

11. baker 12. college chancellor 13. oil driller 14. detective 15. toymaker 16. housecleaner 17. soldier 18. DNA researcher 19. loan officer 20. baseball player

21. athlete 22. personal trainer 23. safecracker 24. barista 25. kangaroo keeper 26. truck driver 27. writer of instruction books 28. teacher 29. justice of the peace 30. peace officer

31. build walls 32. picture framer 33. announcer 34. roadbuilder 35. study amphibians 36. rice grower 37. airport security official 38. thief 39. steal cattle 40. magician

Perfect Marriages

Ella Vader

Born as a DC Comics demigoddess superheroine on December 1941, Wonder Woman recently celebrated her seventy-fifth birthday. I grew up reading about the valiant Amazonian warrior-princess equipped with her Lasso of Truth and indestructible bracelets, sword, and shield.

In addition to being an inspiration to girls—and boys—Wonder Woman is the heroine of a pyrotechnic pun: If Wonder Woman married Howard Hughes and then divorced him and married Henry Kissinger, she'd be (get ready to sing the punch line) "Wonder Hughes Kissinger now!"

Surprising results follow when the right people marry the right people. Here are some fanciful marriages, involving real and fictional personages, between some of my favorite luminaries:

• If Ella Fitzgerald married Darth Vader, she'd be Ella Vader.

• If Rosemary Decamp married William Kunstler, she'd be Rosemarie Decamp Kunstler.

• If Anna Magnani married Martin Mull, she'd be Anna Mull.

• If Imogene Coca married Tom Mix, she'd be Imogene Coca Mix.

• If Jo Ann Worley married Larry Bird, she'd be Jo Ann Worley Bird.

• If Isadora Duncan married Robert Donat, she'd be Isadora Duncan Donat.

• If Annette Bening married Lonzo Ball, she'd be Annette Ball.

• If Ilka Chase married David Seltzer, she'd be Ilka Seltzer.

• If Jodie Foster married Sherlock Holmes, she'd be Jodie Foster Holmes.

• If Bella Abzug married Timothy Bottoms, she'd be Bella Bottoms.

• If Rose Kennedy married George Bush, she'd be Rose Bush.

• If Ellen Burstyn married Red Buttons, she'd be Ellen Burstyn Buttons.

• If J. K. Rowling married Oliver Stone, their children would be Rowling Stones.

• If Meryl Streep married Michael Dukakis, she'd be Meryl Streep Dukakis.

• If Ali McGraw married Jim Kaat, she'd be Ali Kaat.

• If Tuesday Weld married Frederic March's grandson, she'd be Tuesday March the Second.

- If Wynn Everett married Claude Raines, she'd be Wynn Everett Raines.

- If Anita Ekberg married Neil Diamond and then divorced him and married Jack Nicklaus, she'd be Anita Diamond Nicklaus.

- If Olivia Newton-John married Wayne Newton and then divorced him and married Elton John, she'd be Olivia Newton-John Newton John.

- If Liv Ullman married Judge Lance Ito and then divorced him and married Jerry Mathers, she'd be Liv Ito Beaver.

- If Sondra Locke married Elliott Ness and then divorced him and married Herman Munster, she'd be Sondra Locke Ness Munster.

- If Ida Lupino married Dan Rather and then divorced him and married Don Knotts, she'd be Ida Rather Knotts.

- If Karen Black married Chris Rock and then divorced him and married Kenneth Starr, she'd be Karen Black Rock Starr.

- If Sue Grafton married Aaron Burr and then divorced him and married Thomas Mann, she'd be Sue Burr Mann.

- If Phyllis George married Denzel Washington and then divorced him and married Raymond Carver, she'd be Phyllis George Washington Carver.

- If Bo Derek married Richard Nixon and then divorced him and married Clarence Darrow, she'd be Bo N. Darrow.

- If June Allyson married Stevie Wonder and then divorced him and married Edwin Land, she'd be June Allyson Wonder Land.

- If Olivia Wilde married Oscar Wilde and then divorced him and married Kanye West, she'd be Olivia Wilde Wilde West.

- If Judith Light married Jimmy Waite and then divorced him and married Joseph Cotton and then divorced him and married Richard Gere, she'd be Judith Light Waite Cotton Gere.

- If Crystal Gayle married Charlie Chan and then divorced him and married Michael Dell and then divorced him and married Norman Lear, she'd be Crystal Chan Dell Lear.

- If Tippi Hedren married Albert Camus and then divorced him and married Steven Tyler, she'd be Tippi Camus and Tyler, too.

- If Vicki Carr married Martin Mull and then divorced him and married James Caan and then divorced him and married Joey Dee, she'd be Vicki Carr Mull Caan Dee.

- If Gracie Allen married Count Basie and then divorced him and married William Macy and then divorced him and married Spencer Tracy and then divorced him and married Steve Lacy and then divorced him and married Kevin Spacey and then divorced him and married Ben Casey, she'd be Gracie Basie Macy Tracy Lacy Spacey Casey.

- If Ivana Trump married Mister Bean, then divorced him and married King Oscar of Norway, then divorced him and married Mike Myers, and then divorced him and married Anthony Wiener, she'd be Ivana Bean Oscar Myers Wiener!

Nog (Quark's brother on *Star Trek: Deep Space Nine*) has no other name, so he uses it twice when he gets a marriage license and takes the last name of his wife. If he married one of Howard Hughes's wives, then divorced her and married Brynn Thayer, he'd be Nog Nog Hughes Thayer. (I'll knock on the door of knock-knock jokes in a later chapter.)

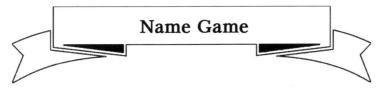

Name Game

Here are a dozen more perfect marriages. For each union supply the married name of the bride:

1. Robin Roberts and Ernie Banks
2. Yoko Ono and Sonny Bono
3. Dolly Parton and Salvador Dali
4. Leslie Caron and Elvis Presley
5. Oprah Winfrey and Depak Chopra
6. Holly Hunter and Elijah Wood
7. Karen Valentine and Dennis Day
8. Rona Barrett and Cecil B. DeMille
9. Anna Magnani and Billy Graham
10. Judy Holliday and Tom Cruise
11. Brooke Shields and Mike Trout
12. Bea Arthur and Sting

Answers

1. Robin Banks 2. Yoko Ono Bono 3. Dolly Dali 4. Leslie Presley 5. Oprah Chopra 6. Holly Wood

7. Karen Valentine Day 8. Rona DeMille 9. Anna Graham 10. Judy Holliday Cruise 11. Brooke Trout 12. Bea Sting

What Have You

May Bee

Have you met the Stein family—Frank N. Stein and Phyllis Stein? Have you met the Teaks—Anne and Bo Teak? Have you met the Manders—Gerry and Sally Mander? Have you met the Clears— Louden and Crystal Clear? And have you met the Hardys—Hale N. and Laurel Ann Hardy?

Have you met the Bee family? There's Honey, May, and Bea Bee. Have you met the Lights? There's Hy and Trudy Light and their sons Al and Flash Light and their daughter Dee Light. Have you met the Grahams? There's Telly and Anna Graham, their son Teddy Graham, and their daughters Candy and Millie Graham.

Have you met the Doe family? There's Tyquon and Dosi Doe and their sons Ron and Wynne Doe and daughters Doe and Lotta Doe. Have you met the Dents? There's Stu and Pru Dent, their son Penn Dent, their daughter Polly Dent, and their Auntie C. Dent. Have you met the Lings? There's Drew and Ceil Ling, their sons Bill, Gig, Phil, Tipp, Todd, and Will Ling and their daughters Belle, Dee, May, and Ming Ling.

Have you met the Dover family? There's Ben and Eileen Dover and their daughters Carrie, Ann, and May Dover, and their sons Bill, Buzz, and Kiel Dover and the quadruplets: Flip, Skip, Tip, and Trip Dover.

And have you met the prolific Lee family? There's Earl and Belle Lee and their sons Abe, Al, Arch, Brock, Bubba, Bull, Court, Coy, Curt, Del, Doyle, Hy, and Phil Lee and their daughters Blithe, Emma, Gay, Ida, Lil, Norma, Ora, Syl, and Val Lee.

Have you heard about Seymour Butts? If you've been a fan of "The Simpsons," you know about Bart's prank phone calls to Moe Syzlak's Tavern. Bart (an anagram of *Brat*) calls up and asks Moe, "Is Seymour Butts there?" Moe turns to his barfly customers and shouts, "Is there a Seymour Butts here? I wanna Seymour Butts." The bar patrons explode with laughter.

Have you heard about the Knights of the Round Table? Sir Cumference, Sir Cular, and Sir Round, the roundest Knights at the Round Table; Sir Loin, the rarest of the knights; Sir Cumcision, who always cut people off; Sir Prize, who always came up with something new; Sir Cus, the foul-mouthed clown; Sir Mount, the brave knight, and Sir Render, the cowardly knight; Sir Rendipitous, who stumbled upon the Holy Grail by sheer luck; Sir Press, the royal censor; Sir Amic, who had feet of clay; Sir Real, the otherworldly knight; Sir Plus and Sir Feit, the over-the-top knights; Sir Reptitious, the secretive knight who always repeated himself; Sir Charge and Sir Tax, the capitalists; Sir Ca, who may or may not have been living at that time; and Sir Lee, the teenage knight.

Have you heard about Ali Kazoo, Amanda B. Reckondwyth, Ana Pology, Anita Mann, Asa Spades, Bart Ender, Bobby Pinn, Buster Bubble, Chester Drawers, Delia Cards, Dan D. Lion, Diane Tameecha, Dee Pend, Dot Matrix, Earl E. Bird, Ella Mentary, Ethel Alcohol, Farah Nuff, Felice Navidad, Flora Klock, Frank Lee Scarlett, Gilda Lily, Gordie N. Knott, Grant Kenyon, Gregor Ian Chant, Haywood Jakissme, Heidi Goseek, Herbie Hind, Hyman Heaven, Ida Cline, Igor Beaver, Ira Peat, Irma Gedden, Jack B. Nimble, Jacques Strap, Jimmy DeLocke, Juan I. Oata, Juan Nightstand, and Kurt Remark?

Have you heard about Lois D. Nominator, Lolly Gag, Lotta Bull, Luke Warm, Macon Whoopie, Maurine Core, Myles Tagoe, Mo Squito, Myra Maines, Nolan Void, Norman D. Beach, Ollie Oxenfree, Paddy Wagon, Percy Snatcher, Polly Wag, Quinn Tuple, Ray Gunn, Ron DeVoo, Roger Overnout, Roxanne Rolls, Ruby Lipps, Sarah Dippity, Saul T. Dogg, Shanda Lear, Sharon Sharalyke, Sue Nora Later, Tamara Morning, Thaddeus Correct, Terry Dactyl, Tina Bopper, Tommy Rott, Wes Sidestory, Willy Nilly, Wilma Puttsink, Winfield Wiper, and Wolfgang Plank?

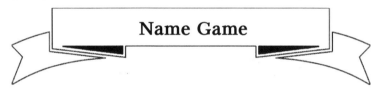

Name Game

Match each first name with each last name to form a word or phrase:

1. Alma	Ball
2. Anna	Beer
3. Archie	Bruptly
4. Belle	Cade
5. Bruno	Curve
6. Bud	Dense
7. Cass	DeSame
8. Chuck	Destruction
9. Crystal	Dout
10. Dee	Eugeste
11. Dick	Fence
12. Don	Fever
13. Eva	Haved

14. Helen	Hawk
15. Hugh	Highwater
16. Jay	Insky
17. Justin	Key
18. Liz	Labor
19. Manuel	Leaky
20. Maura	Log
21. Millie	Long
22. Myles	Mater
23. Noah	Meter
24. Penny	Mongus
25. Peter	Nale
26. Quincy	Nother
27. Rufus	Nyall
28. Rusty	Peace
29. Scarlett	Pelago
30. Shirley	Pincher
31. Tommy	Tater
32. Vera	Tereen
33. Warren	Thyme
34. Welby	Waggen
35. Yetta	Walker

Answers

1. Alma Mater 2. Anna Log 3. Archie Pelago 4. Belle Curve 5. Bruno Beer

6. Bud Inski 7. Cass Cade 8. Chuck Waggen 9. Crystal Ball 10. Dee Nyall

11. Dick Tator 12. Don Key 13. Eva Destruction 14. Helen Highwater 15. Hugh Mongus

16. Jay Walker 17. Justin Thyme 18. Liz Tereen 19. Manuel Labor 20. Maura DeSame

21. Millie Meter 22. Myles Long 23. Noah Fence 24. Penny Pincher 25. Peter Dout

26. Quincy Dense 27. Rufus Leaky 28. Rusty Nale 29. Scarlett Fever 30. Shirley Eugeste

31. Tommy Hawk 32. Vera Bruptly 33. Warren Peace 34. Welby Haved 35. Yetta Nother

Don't Knock
Knock-Knock Jokes

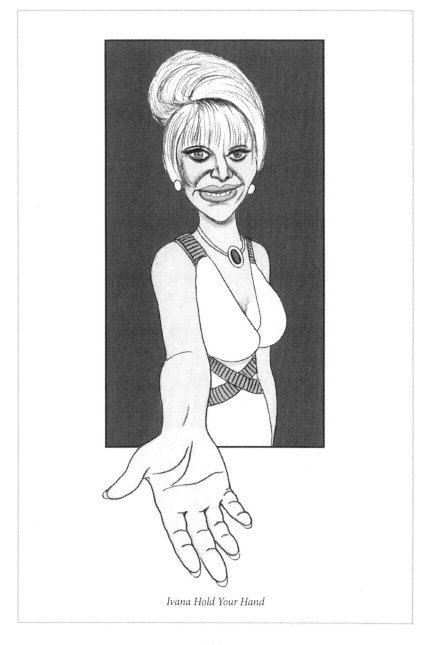

Ivana Hold Your Hand

Knock, knock, knock. Who's there in the name of Beelzebub? . . .
   Knock, knock. Who's there, in the other devil's name? . . .
   Knock, knock, knock. Who's there? Never at quiet!
   —WILLIAM SHAKESPEARE, *MACBETH, Act 2, SCENE 3*

It may be that Shakespeare, who invented so many words and dramatic devices, also pointed the way to the knock-knock joke in the darkest moment of his tragedy *Macbeth*. What we know for sure is that knock-knock jokes have been popular since the late 1920s. Language historian Paul Dickson believes that "the knock-knock joke may be the first truly American formulaic form of humor," one that has become an integral part of our folk culture.

The jokester starts out with "Knock, knock." The second person replies, "Who's there?" The knock-knocker comes back with something like "Dwayne." "Dwayne who?" is the response. Finally, the punch line perpetrates an outrageous pun, such as "Dwayne the bathtub. I'm dwowning!"

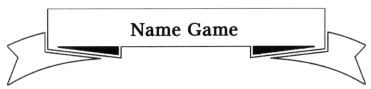

Name Game

Here's a quiz about knock-knock jokes that play exclusively on people's names. Match each name in the list below with the appropriate conclusion that follows.

Knock, knock.
Who's there? . . .

Allyson	Ivan
Amos	King Tut
Andy	Lionel
Ben Hur	Nicholas
Desdemona	Oliver
Eisenhower	Oswald
Harry	Phillip
Henrietta	Sarah
Isabel	Sherwood
Isadore	Walter

Name who?

1. _____quito bit me.
2. _____ bit me again.
3. _____ my bubblegum.
4. _____ locked?
5. _____ to suck your blood.
6. _____ wall carpeting.
7. _____ roar if you don't feed it.
8. _____ like a cold drink.
9. _____ the tub so I can take a bath.
10. _____ an hour, but she hasn't shown up.
11. _____ up, we're late.
12. _____ late for work.
13. _____ troubles will soon be over.
14. _____ doctor in the house?
15. _____ out of order?
16. _____ big dinner and got sick.
17. _____ worth less than a dime.
18. _____ Lisa hang on the wall of this museum?
19. _____ky Fried Chicken.
20. _____ Wonderland.

Answers

1. Amos 2. Andy 3. Oswald 4. Isadore 5. Ivan

6. Walter 7. Lionel 8. Sherwood 9. Phillip 10. Ben Hur

11. Harry 12. Eisenhower 13. Oliver 14. Sarah 15. Isabel

16. Henrietta 17. Nicholas 18. Desdemona 19. King Tut 20. Allyson

The last twenty knock-knock challenges are song lyrics. Again, match each name in the list below with the appropriate conclusion that follows:

Knock, knock. Who's there? . . .

Bessie Mae	Dexter
Bjorn	Flo
Chaim	Ira

Ivana	Rocky
Jose	Sam and Janet
Juan	Shannon
Kay	Shelby
Lorraine	Stan
Meryl Lee	Wayne
Raleigh	Wendy

Name who?

21. _____ can you see?
22. _____ dwops keep falling on my head.
23. _____ mucho.
24. _____ 'round the flag, boys.
25. _____ in the USA.
26. _____ moon hits your eye like a big pizza pie.
27. _____ halls with boughs of holly.
28. _____ comin' around the mountain when she comes.
29. _____ member the night and the Tennessee waltz.
30. _____ evening, you may see a stranger.
31. _____ looking over a four-leaf clover.
32. _____ sera, sera. Whatever will be will be.
33. _____ we roll along.
34. _____ is the loneliest number.
35. _____ by me.
36. _____ hold your hand.
37. _____ bye, baby, on the treetops.
38. _____ gently, sweet Afton.
39. _____ Shannon, harvest moon, up in the sky.
40. _____ in Spain falls mainly on the plain.

Answers

21. Jose 22. Wayne 23. Bessie Mae 24. Raleigh 25. Bjorn

26. Wendy 27. Dexter 28. Shelby 29. Ira 30. Sam and Janet

31. Chaim 32. Kay 33. Meryl Lee 34. Juan 35. Stan

36. Ivana 37. Rocky 38. Flo 39. Shannon 40. Lorraine

Knock, knock. Who's there? Arthur. Arthur who? Arthur any more knock-knock jokes?

Knock, knock. Who's there? Celeste. Celeste Who? Celeste chance we'll have to inflict more knock-knock jokes on you.

Knock, knock. Who's there? Althea. Althea who? Althea later, alligator!

Knock, knock. Who's there? Yoda. Yoda who? Yoda best knock-knock jokester I've ever met!

The Dancing Alphabet

Buster Keaton

Most of the name play you've been hanging out with in this part of the book has been semantic: the humor results from the double meanings of first and last names. Now it's time to have fun with logology, the joy of making the alphabet dance.

An amusing pastime is to string together the first letters of people's names as initials of words in meaningful statements. Lee Iacocca's last name, for example, could be said to represent the first letters of "I Am Chairman Of Chrysler Corporation of America." The name Jason is composed of the first letters of five successive months—July, August, September, October, November. If James Jason were a DJ on FM/AM radio, the first letters of all twelve months would be represented sequentially, starting with June:

J. JASON, DJ, FM/AM

For another example, movie stars Judith Anderson, Béla Lugosi, Julia Roberts, Rosalind Russell, and Blair Underwood, tennis stars Gussie Moran and Guillermo Vilas, golfer Justin Leonard, and Civil War general Ambrose Burnside are among the luminaries whose first and last names together contain all the major vowels—*a, e, i, o*, and *u*. But is there a more compactly voweled surname than that of Grace Metalious, author of the mega-selling small-town exposé *Peyton Place*?

And for yet another example, if you wish to read great *poetry,* just switch the two halves of the word and *try Poe* (Edgar Allan, that is). Other names that qualify as fortunate reversals (words that spell new words when their two halves are reversed) include *Alan/anal, Alton/tonal, Andy/Dyan, Anna/naan, Arden/denar, Arne/near, Boles/lesbo, Cain/Inca, Chou/ouch, Dana/nada, Dane/Neda, Desi/side, Edwin/wined, Eric/icer, Erma/Maer, Ernest/nester, Indra/drain, Kerstin/stinker, Kira/raki, Laver/Verla, Lessing/singles, Levi/vile, Lonny/nylon, Lyman/manly, Lyon/only, Nate/Tena, Olga/gaol, Otto/toot, Pedro/roped, Petri/tripe, Putin/input, Rusty/Tyrus, Ruth/thru, Solly/Lysol, Sonja/Jason, Tesla/slate, Tessa/sates, Vera/rave*, and *Verne/never.*

Exploring a more expansive territory, what do you call a carpenter from Salt Lake City? *A Mormon Nailer.* And what do you call an elderly sadist? *Whip Van Wrinkle.* The answers to the two riddles switch the first letters in the name of American author Norman Mailer and the name of Rip Van Winkle, a character created by another American author, Washington Irving. That kind of transposition is called a spoonerism, eponymously named after the Rev. William Archibald Spooner, whom you met in an earlier chapter, "Immortal Mortals."

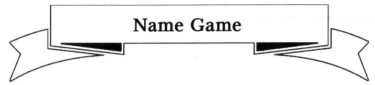

Name Game

Here's a list of what look like first and last names. Switch the initial sounds of these names and you'll discover an aggregation of famous names. For example, *Gil Bates* turns into *Bill Gates* and *Polly Darton* into *Dolly Parton*. If you experience trouble understanding a spoonerism, it may help to say it out loud.

1. Ben Kerns	6. Garvin Mae	11. Larry Garson	16. Millie Barton
2. Berle Paley	7. Jetta Ames	12. Mackie Jason	17. Nellie Wilson
3. Candy Owen	8. Jody Brenner	13. Mary Culligan	18. Nick Dixon
4. Carrie Ling	9. Kellen Heller	14. Mary Gore	19. Ricky Mooney
5. Gary Holden	10. Ken Barson	15. Merrie Payson	20. Robby Biggs

Answers

1. Ken Burns 2. Pearl Bailey 3. Andy Cohen 4. Larry King 5. Harry Golden

6. Marvin Gaye 7. Etta James 8. Brody Jenner 9. Helen Keller 10. Ben Carson

11. Gary Larson 12. Jackie Mason 13. Kerry Mulligan 14. Gary Moore 15. Perry Mason

16. Billy Martin 17. Willie Nelson 18. Dick Nixon 19. Mickey Rooney 20. Bobby Riggs

I, your wordaholic author, was born with a silver spoonerism in my mouth, so I'll now shower you with even more spectacular reversals.

Do you know that *Sarah Palin* goes *parasailin'; Al Gore* creates spoonerisms *galore; James Taylor tames* his *jailer; Marcia Gaye Harden* cultivates, when life grows *harsh, a May garden;* and with his enchanted sword, *Harry Potter* can *parry hotter*? But that's only *when your senses* say *Señor Wences.*

Does *Justin Trudeau trust in judo*? Does *Ted Rose* have *red toes*? Does *Jack Benny back Jenny*? Does *Jack Warden whack Jordan*? Does *Jack Sock sack a jock*? Does *Dennis Miller menace Diller*? Does *Bruce Lee* find some *loose brie*? Does *Francis Scott Key* let off *Kansas scot free*? And does *Buster Keaton* study American history and read about *Custer beaten*?

Does *Jude Law* have a *lewd jaw*? Does *Patti LaBelle* wear a *batty lapel*? Does *Dinah Shore shine a door*? Does *Rob Lowe lob roe*? Does *Gene Kelly* make a *keen jelly*? Does *John Kelly con jelly* and *John Kerry con Jerry*? And does *Will Shortz shill warts*?

Does *Beverly Sills* ring *silvery bells*? Does *Bill Maher* drink at a *mill bar*? Does *Bob Marley mob barley*? Does *Thomas Mann* admire his *mama's tan*? Does *Tom Mix* know that his *mom ticks*? And did *Booth Tarkington* name his dog *Tooth Barkington*?

Does *John Wayne* date *wan Jane*? Does *Dean Martin* do some *mean dartin'*? Does *Barry White* avoid a *wary bite*? Does *Laverne Cox* use *cavern locks*? Does *Lana Turner tan a learner*? Does *Kevin Hart* ride in a *heaven cart*? Does *Dan Brown* keep his *bran down*? Does *Sonny Fox* wear *funny sox*? And does *Hale Boggs bail hogs*?

Is *Steven Pinker* a *peevin' stinker*? Is *Howard Keel* a *coward heel*? Is *Tony Bennett* a *bony Tenet*? Is *Cole Porter* a *pole courter*? Is *Brian Cox* a *cryin' box*? Is *Herman Melville* a *merman* from *Hellville*? Is *Joan Kroc* a *crone jock*? Is *Maggie Smith* a *saggy myth*? Is *Will Smith* a *swill myth*? Is *Fred Durst* someone we should *dread first*? Is *Keenan Wynn* busy *weanin' kin*? And is *Scott Pruitt*'s opinion of marijuana *Pot*? *Screw it!*

Turning to the world of sports: Is it true that *James Blake blames Jake* and that *Dave Winfield waived infield* practice? Is *Ryan Leaf* a *lyin' reef*? Did *Bart Starr start* a *Bar*? Does *Dan Fouts fan doubts*? Does *Randall Cunningham* hold a *candle* to a *running ham*? Does *Brian Kelly* have a *cryin' belly*? Does *Tracy Austin* prefer something *racy tossed in*? And, hey, I've known *Mike Tyson* since he was a *tyke, my son*.

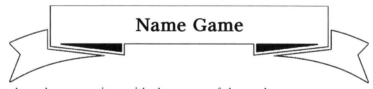

Name Game

Match each spoonerism with the name of the real person:

1. ban drown	Benny Hill
2. boozin' soil	Bob Fosse
3. brew lock	Brad Pitt
4. bris crown	Cheryl Ford
5. coward hose sell	Chris Brown
6. feral shored	Dan Brown

7.	fob bossy	Doctor Seuss
8.	henny bill	Harry Truman
9.	pack jar	Howard Cosell
10.	pad Brit	Jack Parr
11.	rally side	Knute Rockne
12.	root knock knee	Lou Brock
13.	socked her deuce	Mark Spitz
14.	spark mitts	Sally Ride
15.	tarry human	Susan Boyle

Answers

1. Dan Brown 2. Susan Boyle 3. Lou Brock 4. Chris Brown 5. Howard Cosell

6. Cheryl Ford 7. Bob Fosse 8. Benny Hill 9. Jack Paar 10. Brad Pitt

11. Sally Ride 12. Knute Rockne 13. Doctor Seuss 14. Mark Spitz 15. Harry Truman

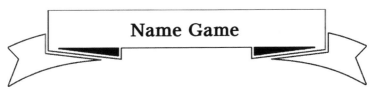

Name Game

What characteristic do the following words share?: *any, arty, beady, cagey, cutie, decay, easy, empty, envy, essay, excel, excess, icy, ivy, kewpie, seedy, teepee,* and *ziti.* Turns out that each word is cobbled from the sounds of two letters—*NE, RT, BD, KG, QT, DK, EZ, MT, NV, SA, XL, XS, IC, IV, QP, CD, TP,* and *ZT.* We call such words grammagrams.

Try your hand at some word fun with first names that consist of only letter sounds. Identify the first name of each real or fictional person described below:

1. He was a 2017 Academy Award winner.
2. She played Carmela Soprano.
3. They feature roast beef.
4. She was one of the Beverly Hillbillies.
5. She's a country singer for whom "Love Hurts."
6. He was a Fijian golfer.
7. She's a singer and songwriter and "One of the Boys."

8. She's a talk show host.

9. He's a superstar white rapper.

10. She was the Belle of Amherst.

Answers

1. Casey (KC) Affleck 2. Edie (ED) Falco 3. Arby (RB, which stands for the founding Raffel brothers) 4. Elly (LE) Mae Clampett 5. Emmy (ME) Lou Harris

6. Vijay (VJ) Singh 7. Katy (KT) Perry 8. Ellen (LN) DeGeneres 9. Eminem (MNM) 10. Emily (MLE) Dickinson

Anagram Crackers

William Shakespeare = I swear he's like a lamp

As you learned earlier in this book, an anagram is a rearrangement of all the letters in a word or sentence to make a new and penetrating word or sentence. *Word Ways* editor Ross Eckler electronically riffled through more than ninety million names in U.S. telephone directories to find examples of the following listings, in which each first and last name house the same letters:

Roland Arnold	Dale Deal	Neal Lane	Leon Noel
Ronald Arnold	Edna Dean	Earl Lear	Erich Reich
Debra Bader	Gary Gray	Amy May	Eric Rice
Albert Bartel	Leah Hale	Romeo Moore	Arnold Roland
Debra Beard	Lena Lane	Norma Moran	Ronald Roland
Marc Cram			Lewis Wiles

Of Hebrew origin, the name *Daniel* means "God is my judge." Here's a little ditty in which each of the twelve lines is composed of just the six letters in the name *Daniel*:

> An idle
> Lead-in
> Denali
> Ad line:
> DANIEL,
> Nailed
> In deal
> (i.e., land
> In dale),
> Led in a
> Denial
> And lie.

For centuries, name players have been anagramming the names of the famous and infamous, from historical personages:

Adam and Eve	DAD, EVEN A MA
Adolf Hitler	HATED FOR ILL
Alexander the Great	GENERAL TAXED EARTH.
Daniel Boone	IN LONE ABODE

139

Eleanor Roosevelt	ROLE: TO SERVE ALONE
Florence Nightingale	FLIT ON, CHEERING ANGEL.
Grover Cleveland	GOVERN, CLEVER LAD.
Horatio Nelson	LO, NATION'S HERO
Jacqueline Kennedy Onassis	IS AS QUEENLY ON DECK WITH JEANS
Margaret Thatcher	MEG, THE ARCH TARTAR
Martin Luther King	LINE MARKING TRUTH
Napoleon Bonaparte	NO. APPEAR NOT ON ELBA.
Saddam Hussein	HISSED, "DAMN U.S.A."
Spiro Agnew	GROW A SPINE.
Ulysses Simpson Grant	SURPASSINGNESS MY LOT.

to scientists:

Albert Einstein	TEN ELITE BRAINS
Charles Darwin	CRANIAL, SHREWD
Madam Curie	RADIUM CAME.
Sir Michael Faraday	AHA! I CLARIFY DREAMS.
Sir Isaac Newton	WITS: I CAN REASON.

to writers:

Adeline Virginia Woolf	I,A LOVING WIFE, I, LEONARD
Charles Dickens	CHEER SICK LANDS.
Ernest Hemingway	WHERE'S MY NEAT GIN?
Henry Wadsworth Longfellow	WON HALF THE NEW WORLD'S GLORY
Henry David Thoreau	A VERY HIDDEN AUTHOR
Miguel Cervantes de Saavedra	GAVE US A DAMNED CLEVER SATIRE
Oliver Wendell Holmes	HE'LL DO IN MELLOW VERSE.
Oscar Wilde	I LACE WORDS.
Ralph Waldo Emerson	PERSON WHOM ALL READ
Richard Lederer	RIDDLER REACHER
Salman Rushdie	DARE SHUN ISLAM.
Samuel Taylor Coleridge	DELOUSE MY ALLEGORIC ART.
Sir Walter Scott	LAST SCOT WRITER
William Butler Yeats	ART, BEAUTY WILL SMILE.

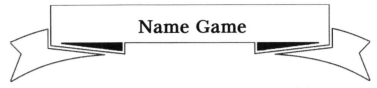

Name Game

Here are eight anagrams of the first and last names of the most famous writer who ever set quill to parchment. Who is he?

HAS WILL A PEER, I ASK ME.

WE ALL MAKE HIS PRAISE.

I SWEAR HE'S LIKE A LAMP.

WISE MALE. AH, I SPARKLE.

HEAR ME, AS I WILL SPEAK.

I 'LL MAKE A WISE PHRASE.

AH, I SPEAK A SWELL RIME.

I AM A WEAKISH SPELLER.

Answer

William Shakespeare

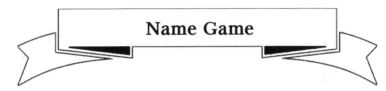

Name Game

Match each first name with the first name that is its anagram, as in Ernie-Irene and Dolly-Lloyd:

1. Alice	Celia
2. Allen	Christina
3. Amy	Cornelia
4. Andy	Dyan
5. Ann	Edna
6. Arden	Ira
7. Ari	Jean
8. Arnold	Marina
9. Avram	Marva
10. Caroline	May
11. Christian	Merle
12. Dean	Miley

13. Dorothea	Myra
14. Elmer	Nan
15. Emily	Nedra
16. Jane	Nella
17. Jason	Noel
18. Leon	Roland
19. Marian	Sonja
20. Mary	Theodora

Answers

1. Celia 2. Nella 3. May 4. Dyan 5. Nan
6. Nedra 7. Ira 8. Roland (and Ronald) 9. Marva 10. Cornelia
11. Christina 12. Edna (and Dane) 13. Theodora 14. Merle 15. Miley
16. Jean 17. Sonja 18. Noel 19. Marina 20. Myra

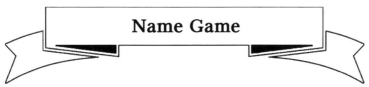

Name Game

Born Theodosia Burr Goodman, Theda Bara, known as The Vamp, was a wildly popular star of silent films. Her stage name turned out to be an anagram of ARAB DEATH, and her Fox Studio publicists claimed inaccurately that she was the daughter of an Arab sheik. Being Jewish, she wasn't.

Match each entertainer's name with each anagram:

1. A "CATCH THEM WOMEN" GUY	Alec Guinness
2. ACTOR INDEED!	Beverly Sills
3. A MANIC JOKES	Clint Eastwood
4. FINE IN TORN JEANS	Eddie Cantor
5. GENUINE CLASS	Elvis Aaron Presley
6. OLD WEST ACTION	Jackie Mason
7. ONE COOL DANCE MUSICIAN	Jennifer Aniston
8. SEEN ALIVE? SORRY, PAL.	Madonna Louise Ciccone
9. SILVERY BELLS	Matthew McConaughey
10. SO I'M CUTER.	Tom Cruise

Answers

1. Matthew McConaughey 2. Eddie Cantor 3. Jackie Mason 4. Jennifer Aniston 5. Alec Guinness

6. Clint Eastwood 7. Madonna Louise Ciccone 8. Elvis Aaron Presley 9. Beverly Sills 10. Tom Cruise

Palindromania

Now that you've explored the spooneristic and anagrammatical wonders of names, it's time to enter the great Palin-dome of Palindromes.

A palindrome is a word, word row, sentence, or longer statement that communicates the same message when the letters in it are read in reverse order. For example, anyone who would impugn the reputation of the former governor of Alaska and 2008 Republican vice presidential candidate Sarah Palin would be out to HARASS SARAH. Read the two words forward and backward and you'll see that they form a palindrome, as well as—ta da!—a Palin drome!

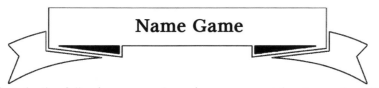

Name Game

What do the following names have in common: Ada, Anna, Asa, Bob, Elle, Eve, Gig, Hannah, Lil, Mim, Nan, Otto, and Viv?

Answer

They are all palindromes.

It may be that the very first sentence ever spoken was a palindrome. We are told that the Deity plunged Adam into a deep sleep prior to extracting a rib wherewith to make him a helpmeet. When he awoke, Adam, to his amazement, found Eve (possessing the first palindromic name) by his side. Having no one to introduce him, he politely bowed and spake (in English, of course): MADAM, I'M ADAM:

Name Me Man

Backward and forward, as you will perceive,
Read Adam's first greeting to dear Mother Eve:
MADAM, I'M ADAM. Now we can conceive
That her answer was simply: EVE, MAD ADAM, EVE.

In addition to the names of celebrated personages, palindromes incorporate the likes of plain old Dennis and Edna:
DENNIS AND EDNA SINNED.

And they're not the only transgressors:

DENNIS, NELL, EDNA, MARVA, LEON, NEDRA, ANITA, ROLF, NORA, ALICE, CAROL, LEO, JANE, REED, DENA, DALE, BASIL, RAE, PENNY, LANA, DAVE, DENNY, LENA, IDA, BERNADETTE, BEN, RAY, LILA, NINA, JO, IRA, MARA, ANNE, NORAH, SELA, GAIA, MABLE, MINA, RAE, BARBA, ROLLO, PAM, ADA, FLORA, TINA, NELL, ETTA, MARY, META, NOEL, FLO, DOT, TOM, ASA, RITA, NAN, IDA, TED, ANA, ESME, HANNAH, EM, SEAN, ADE, TAD, INA, NAT, IRA, SAM, OTTO, DOLF, LEO, NATE, MYRA, MATT, ELLEN, ANITA, ROLF, ADAM, APOLLO, RABRA, BEA, RANI, MELBA, MAIA, GALE, SHARON, ENNA, ARA, MA-RIO, JAN, INA, LILY, ARNE, BETTE, DAN, REBA, DIANE, LYNN, ED, EVA, DANA, LYNNE, PEARL, ISABEL, ADA, NED, DEE, RENA, JOEL, LORA, CECIL, AARON, FLORA, TINA, ARDEN, NOEL, AVRAM, AND ELLEN SINNED!

To make up a palindrome is a Herculean labor because the vocabulary available to the task is severely limited. Most words simply can't be bent into a shape that can be included in a push me-pull you palindrome. Nonetheless, I am pleased to display a treasure trove of famous-name palindromes. First, have a look at a pyramid of single names only:

DIOR DROID

NEMO WOMEN

POSE AS AESOP.

SAD, I'M MIDAS.

XERXES: EX-REX

NO 'X' IN NIXON

NO, I DID DIDION.

Y'ALL, I'M MILLAY

SUIT NO PONTIUS.

RED LENIN ELDER

O. J., NAB A BANJO.

A SANTA AT NASA.

I, PLATO, TOTAL PI.

NO, SMASH SAMSON.

I'M RUNNIN', NURMI.

VANNA, WANNA "V"?

CAMUS SEES SUMAC.

NOW SUNUNU'S WON.

DRACULA VALU-CARD

CAIN: A MONOMANIAC

NO, SID. AM I MADISON?

PAGANINI: DIN IN A GAP

NOT LENNON 'N' ELTON.

ROB A GEM? ME? GABOR?

AH! A BAHA'I! AHAB! AHA!

BAR ARAFAT, A FAR ARAB.

ERROL'S PAL SLAPS LORRE.

GOD, ASTOR TROTS A DOG.

I YAM POPEYE, POP. MAY I?

PURE VENUS: SUN EVER UP

NEMO, WE REVERE WOMEN.

HELL, ATTILA LIT TALL, EH?

SO MAY APOLLO PAY AMOS.

NO, HAL. I LED DELILAH ON.

MAN, OPRAH'S SHARP ON A.M.

NORIEGA CASTS A CAGE: IRON.

I DID NOT RUB BURTON, DID I?

DRAT SADDAM, A MAD DASTARD.

SIR, I SOON SAW I WAS NO OSIRIS.

TO LAST, CARTER RETRACTS A LOT.

REPORT IT, ROPER. PULL A GALLUP.

DRAW, O CAESAR. ERASE A COWARD.

AH, ARISTIDES OPPOSED IT, SIR. AHA!

EVA, CAN I POSE AS AESOP IN A CAVE?

RAW-FIST CAPONE: "NO PACTS IF WAR!"

NO HAM CAME, SIR. RISE, MACMAHON.

YAWN. MADONNA FAN? NO DAMN WAY!

MANET TASTES SAP ASSETS AT TEN A.M.

NO, SIRRAH. DELIVER REVILED HARRISON.

DEPARDIEU, GO RAZZ A ROGUE I DRAPED.

EH? DID ZORRO GIVE VIGOR, ROZ? DID HE?

SET ARC. OSTRACIZE FEZ. I CART SOCRATES.

SUMS ARE NOT SET AS A TEST ON ERASMUS.

SIS, ASK COSTNER TO NOT RENT SOCKS "AS IS."

NOW ALL ARE NEGATIVE, EVITA; GENERAL LAW ON.

BERYL, NOSY VISIONARY CYRANO IS IVY'S ONLY REB.

SO MAY OBADIAH, EVEN IN NINEVEH, AID A BOY, AMOS.

MAD ZEUS, NO LIVE DEVIL DEIFIED, LIVED EVIL ON SUEZ DAM.

SALADIN ENROBES A BARONESS, SENORA, BASE-BORN ENID, ALAS.

DEER FLEE FREEDOM IN OREGON? NO, GERONIMO. DEER FEEL FREED.

Finally, climb to the pinnacle of palindromes, in which both the first and last names are preserved by at least an initial. The final three palindromes are so pyrotechnic in length that they each take up two lines:

OH NO! DON HO!

ONO OK, O YOKO ONO?

R. E. LEE, POTATO PEELER

TO IDI AMIN: I'M A IDIOT.

LISA BONET ATE NO BASIL.

LEG, NET OILER, ELIOT ENGEL

'TIS BURL IVES AS EVIL RUBS IT.

TARZAN RAISED DESI ARNAZ' RAT.

TONI TENNILLE FELL IN NET. I, NOT.

LIAM NEESON DEIFIED NO SEEN MAIL.

WON'T I, PATTI PAGE, GAP IT, TAP IT NOW?

NO, MEL GIBSON IS A CASINO'S BIG LEMON.

DARE DICK LEDERER RE: RED ELK CIDER AD.

E. BORGNINE DRAGS DAD'S GARDENING ROBE.

ED, I SAW HARPO MARX RAM OPRAH W. ASIDE.

HAKEEM OLAJUWON'S NOW UJA! LO! MEEK! AH!

HE'S A CARAMEL IN NIGER, DAKAR—A BUM IN SOHO—

HOSNI MUBARAK, A DREG IN NILE MARACAS, EH?

OH, WE TALK LAWSUIT. NO PETAL, I PRESUME, RIPS A TACO CAT.

ASPIRE, MUSER, PILATE, PONTIUS, WALK LATE. WHO?

T. ELIOT, TOP BARD, NOTES PUTRID TANG EMANATING. IS SAD.

I'D ASSIGN IT A NAME: "GNAT DIRT UPSET ON DRAB POT TOILET."

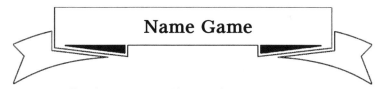

Name Game

My Aunt Matilda is a very peculiar relative, a woman of strong likes and dislikes when it comes to people's names. For example, my Aunt Matilda likes Bob but not Bill, Hannah but not Hans, and Otto but not Octavia. It took me awhile to realize that Aunt Matilda likes names that are palindromic.

For another example, my Aunt Matilda likes Damon but not David, Delbert but not Della, and Dennis but not Denzel. In this case, my Aunt Matilda prefers names that, when reversed, spell words—here *nomad, trebled,* and *sinned.*

In fact, all of my Aunt Matilda's steadfast preferences for names can be explained by the patterns of letters and sounds in those names. You can test your ability to see patterns by trying to figure out why my Aunt Matilda's likes some names and turns her nose up at others. Examine each cluster and state the reason for Aunt Matilda's preferences.

1. Aunt Matilda likes Dennis but not Denise, Ellen but not Elise, and Henrietta but not Henry.

2. Aunt Matilda likes Aaron but not Erin, Lee but not Leon, and Brooklyn but not Lyn.

3. Aunt Matilda likes Glenn but not Glenda, Jane but not Janet, and Dane but not Dana.

4. Aunt Matilda likes Eve but not Adam, Ira but not Myra, and Roy but not Rachel.

5. Aunt Matilda likes Bobo but not Bob, Cici but not Cecil, and Deedy but not Deirdre.

6. Aunt Matilda likes Amos but not Alice, Beatrice but not Bernard, and Irene but not Irma.

7. Aunt Matilda likes Leon but not Leila, Nella but not Ella, and Delbert but not Bert.

8. Aunt Matilda likes Barbara but not Jennifer, Phillip but not Phyllis, and Samantha but not Samuel.

9. Aunt Matilda likes David but not Donna, Eugene but not Eugenia, and Miriam but not Mary.

10. Aunt Matilda likes Ambrose Burnside but not Stonewall Jackson, Julia Roberts but not Julianne Moore, and Rosalind Russell, but not Rosie O'Donnell.

Answers

My Aunt Matilda likes 1. names that contain double consonants 2. names that contain double vowels 3. one-syllable names 4. three-letter names 5. rhyming names (reduplications)

6. names that start with long vowels 7. names that become other names when their letters are reversed 8. names in which only one vowel appears repeatedly 9. names that begin and end with the same letter 10. names that include the vowels *a*, *e*, *i*, *o*, and *u*.

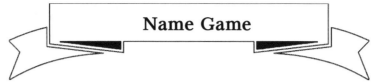

Name Game

English is a highly possessive language: We have so many expressions concocted from the formula "whose what" that we can run the gamut from A to Z many times. Starting at A, we have *Adam's apple*, so called because many men, but few women, exhibit a bulge of laryngeal cartilage in front of their throats. According to male-dominated folklore, Eve swallowed her apple without care or residue, while a chunk of the fruit stuck in the throat of the misled but basically honest Adam.

Ending with Z, we have Zeno's paradoxes, a series of eight brain busters posed by the Greek philosopher Zeno of Elea (495–430 B.C.). The most famous of Zeno's posers goes like this: Achilles sees a tortoise moving slowly ahead in the distance and sets out to catch up with it. But when he reaches point A, where he first saw the tortoise, the animal has moved ahead to point B. And when Achilles gets to B, the tortoise has progressed to point C. Therefore, no matter how determinedly or swiftly Achilles races ahead, he can never catch up with the tortoise.

I'm confident that you can catch up with an exhibition of twenty "whose whats" that involve human names. Provide the missing possessive name for each compound that follows, as in Murphy's Law:

1. Achilles _____   6. Hobson's _____
2. Custer's _____   7. Noah's _____
3. Davy Jones' _____   8. Orion's _____
4. Frankenstein's _____   9. Pandora's _____
5. Halley's _____   10. Rubik's _____

Now a bonus section for book lovers. The titles of many works of literature also adhere to the "whose what" pattern. Supply the names that kick off each literary title below, as in Alice's Adventures in Wonderland:

11. _____'s Baby   16. _____'s Elegy
12. _____'s Body   17. _____'s Lover
13. _____'s Cabin   18. _____'s Progress
14. _____'s Choice   19. _____'s Travels
15. _____'s Complaint   20. _____'s Web

Answers

1. heel 2. last stand 3. locker 4. monster 5. Comet 6. choice 7. ark
8. belt 9. box 10. Cube

11. Rosemary 12. John Brown 13. Uncle Tom 14. Sophie 15. Portnoy
16. Gray 17. Lady Chatterley 18. Pilgrim 19. Gulliver 20. Charlotte